The Black Boys Uprising of 1765

The Black Boys Uprising of 1765

Traders, Troops & "Rioters" during Pontiac's War

Dan Guzy

The Conococheague Institute

The Black Boys Uprising of 1765
Traders, Troops & "Rioters" during Pontiac's War
©2014 Dan Guzy

Published in the United States of America by

The Conococheague Institute
12995 Bain Road
Mercersburg, PA 17236
Phone: (717) 328-3467
Fax: (717) 328-2800
info@cimlg.org
www.cimlg.org
www.cimlg.org/blog
www.facebook.com/conococheagueinstitute

Front cover images:
Top, Fort Loudoun. *Lower left,* Black Boys rebellion marker. A registered trademark ® of the Pennsylvania Historical and Museum Commission and the marker is copyright protected. Used with permission. *Lower center,* Indian attack on settlers (Egle, *An Illustrated History of the Commonwealth of Pennsylvania,* 1880). *Lower right,* Portrait believed to be Colonel James Smith in old age (Courtesy of the Eva G. Farris Special Collections, W. Frank Steely Library, Northern Kentucky University).

Unless otherwise credited, all photos in this book were taken by the author.

Table of Contents

Preface

In preparing for a 2015 bus tour to commemorate the 250th anniversary of the Conococheague Black Boys and their uprising, I found there was much material to draw from. However, the primary sources were scattered collections of letters, depositions, meeting minutes, newspaper articles, and an autobiography that often covered events out of chronological order. The secondary sources that attempted to pull this material together usually did so in very condensed summaries, and set them in context of other, broader themes. There was no complete, detailed story of what happened during the Conococheague uprising of 1765, and that showed the influence of provincial politics, and military and diplomatic actions during Pontiac's War.

When Leighton Wolffe, president of the Conococheague Institute's board of directors, suggested that I write a book on the uprising, I quickly agreed with hopes of filling that void.

Dan Guzy
2014

Acknowledgements

I thank Leighton Wolffe, president of The Conococheague Institute's board of directors and Heather Wade, the Institute's executive director, for their encouragement and support in preparing this book. I also thank librarian Dr. Joan McKean, Tom Finucane, and others at the Institute for their help, Jill Schooley who drew its map, and Diane Hanse and Sharon Nelson of the Greenwood Muse Ensemble who provided the music notation presented in Appendix 1.

I am also grateful to local historians Calvin Bricker and John Thompson who advised me in my initial research, and who, along with Tim Rockwell, Glenn Cordell, and Anna Rotz, reviewed and contributed to the first draft of this book.

Lastly, I thank my granddaughters, Hannah and Sammy, for reminding me that "history is so much fun."

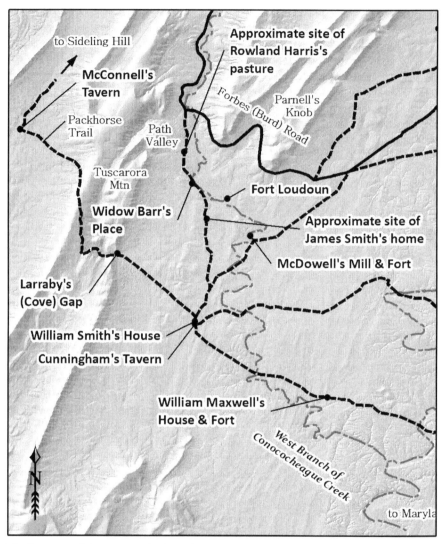

The location of the sites marked on this map are fairly well known. However, typically the routes of historic roads and paths between sites are not known with any precision and there may be disagreements between various estimates of routes. For example, some authors have concluded that Forbes' and Burd's Road(s) hugged the foot of Parnell's and Jordan's Knobs as show on our map. Other authors have assumed that Burd's Road went directly to Fort McDowell and Forbes' Road went directly to Fort Loudoun. We have chosen to base our estimates of routes on the map in Wilbur Nye's book (see References), but made some adjustments to fit sites not shown on Nye's.

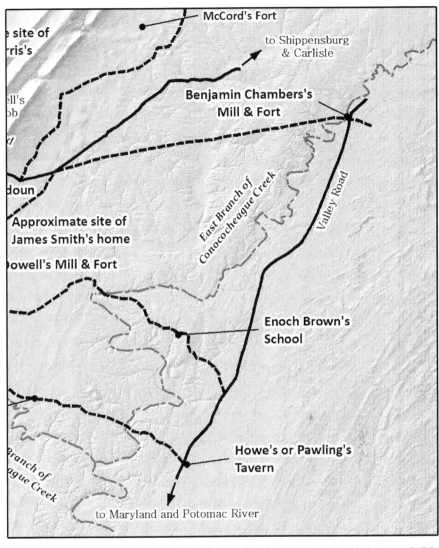

McCord's Fort

site of
ris's

to Shippensburg
& Carlisle

ell's
bb
d

Benjamin Chambers's
Mill & Fort

doun

East Branch of
Conococheague Creek

Valley Road

Approximate site of
James Smith's home

owell's Mill & Fort

Enoch Brown's
School

Branch of
ague Creek

Howe's or Pawling's
Tavern

to Maryland and Potomac River

Map Created in ArcGIS by Jill L. Schooley, GISP

Introduction

The Conococheague uprising of 1765 began as protests and attacks by local settlers against traders they believed were bringing arms and ammunition to the Ohio Indians—those tribes who killed and captured family members and neighbors the previous year, and in other years before that. The Indian raids in the Conococheague settlement had ceased by 1765 with ongoing peace negotiations. However, a formal peace treaty had not been reached in the first part of the year and Pennsylvania law still prohibited the trade of weapons to enemy Indians. In March, an organized Conococheague group known as "the Black Boys," because they blackened their faces as disguises, intercepted and destroyed a shipment of Indian trade goods to ensure that the law remained enforced.

When the British troops at Fort Loudoun gave aid and protection to the traders, and arrested protestors and took their guns, the conflict soon became one of local inhabitants versus the local troops. Pressured by the British army command and Philadelphia merchants, Pennsylvania's governor attempted legal means to bring order and place the "banditti" and "rioters" on trial, but a strong solidarity among the frontiersman and several of the local magistrates prevented that from happening.

The Black Boys' ongoing inspections and regulation of private and military convoys on local roads, along with more confrontations with Fort Loudoun troops, further outraged their opponents. But the Conococheague men bravely stayed together and continued their resistance.

Chapter 1

Indians, Settlers and the
French & Indian War

Pioneers first settled along Conococheague (rhymes with "Monica Jig") Creek and its two branches in the 1730s. Today this creek runs through Franklin County, Pennsylvania and Washington County, Maryland as it drains into the Potomac River. But in 1765 the two colonies' westernmost counties—Cumberland County in Pennsylvania and Frederick County in Maryland—claimed the Conococheague settlement at the southwest end of the Cumberland Valley.

When Benjamin Chambers settled at the confluence of Falling Spring Creek and the East Branch of Conococheague Creek around 1730, he opened the way for others to purchase or squat on the surrounding lands. At that time, few if any Native Americans were there. Hundreds of Indian sites have been identified in the Conococheague drainage region, causing some early writers to incorrectly assume there must have been natives in villages to greet the white settlers as they moved in. However, modern archeological assessments of these sites and their artifacts found that only one site, Ebbert Spring, south of Greencastle, had any evidence of European contact. The rest have been determined to be prehistoric sites.

There are but few anecdotal accounts of interactions between Indians and whites in the Conococheague settlement prior to the French & Indian War

(1755-1763). Historians such as James D. Rice concluded that after Europeans first arrived in America, Indians came to the area only to hunt or to pass through on their warpath between northern and southern tribes.[1]

When William Penn and his Quaker followers founded Pennsylvania in 1681, they respected the native tribes and obtained lands through purchase rather than conquest. Treaties and conferences involving gift exchanges ensured good relationships. After William Penn's death in 1718, the new proprietors, Penn's heirs, relied on James Logan and Conrad Weiser to implement an Indian policy recognizing the Six Nations of the Iroquois as having dominion over other tribes. The Iroquois negotiated and treated with the Pennsylvanians and in return controlled the various tribes that established villages along the eastern shore of the Susquehanna River. This diplomacy maintained a lasting peace in Pennsylvania, even when the neighboring Maryland and Virginia colonies had conflicts and wars with Indians.

The fur and hide export industry was highly profitable to colonists. The Indians supplying such skins became very dependent on European goods. They traded for iron and brass kettles, hoes and axes, knives and hatchets, glass beads, blankets, needles and thread, woolen cloth, ribbons and all sorts of clothing, including hats, matchcoats, shirts, stockings, and shoes. Rum brought both joy and misery to them. Most important were the guns, gunpowder, and lead for bullets that the Indians relied on for food, furs, and warfare with other tribes. So while the Indians periodically moved farther and farther west to avoid the continuing encroachment of white settlers and their livestock into Indian hunting grounds and cornfields, they kept fur-trading relations with those who could bring the goods they wanted.

Present giving was an important part of Native American culture. The status of a chief or rising member of a tribe was based heavily on what he gave to others rather than what he owned. Indian chiefs came to expect generous gifts from the colonial governments at their conferences, gifts that they in turn would redistribute within their tribes.

Generally, British goods were cheaper and better made than those offered by the French traders of Canada. That helped keep Indians connected to the British colonial governments and British fur traders. Irish-born George Croghan, whom historians have dubbed "the king of Pennsylvanian traders," developed a powerful influence with western tribes. He would play a key diplomatic role during the French & Indian and Pontiac's wars. However, the actions of Croghan and his secret partners would also spark the Conococheague uprising of 1765.

The Shawnee Indians considered the Delaware (Lenape) to be their "grandfathers" and both nations shared the Algonquian language. By the early 1700s, the Delawares had moved from their villages on the tidal Delaware River and the Shawnees had moved into Pennsylvania along the eastern shore of the Susquehanna River. By the 1730s, many in those tribes had moved up along the Juniata River and beyond, into new villages on the Allegheny and Ohio Rivers in far western Pennsylvania. These tribes never settled in the Conococheague area, but their warriors would later brutally attack the Conococheague settlement, as well as other frontier regions of Pennsylvania, Maryland and Virginia during the French & Indian and Pontiac's wars. Fear that these Indians would strike again in 1765, if re-armed by George Croghan and other traders, was an underlying cause of the Conococheague uprising.

West Branch of Conococheague Creek, near Fort Loudoun

3

Benjamin Chamber's farm and mill in what is now Chambersburg were firsts in the region. Soon afterward, James Black settled near the Conococheague's West Branch and built a trading post and mill on what is now called Johnston's Run. In 1759, William Smith bought Black's properties. The stream became "Smith's Run" and "Black's Town" became known as "Smith's Town" or "Squire Smith's Town." Later the town was re-named "Mercersburg" after Hugh Mercer, who had been a local doctor and a hero of the French & Indian and Revolutionary wars.[2]

William Smith was born in Chester County, Pennsylvania and moved to the Conococheague settlement sometime before 1748, the year he became a lieutenant in Colonel Benjamin Chamber's militia regiment. In 1757, Smith was one of the new magistrates (justices of the peace) of Cumberland County—a position he would hold until the governor stripped him of that office in 1766 because of his role in the Conococheague uprising. William Smith married Mary Smith, his cousin and sister of James Smith. William Smith and his younger cousin/brother-in-law, James Smith, were the primary leaders of the Conococheague uprising.[3]

The Pennsylvania government encouraged the migration of settlers into the Conococheague region, partly to secure the colony's southern border then in dispute with Maryland, and partly to form the southernmost of Cumberland Valley settlements serving as a buffer between eastern Pennsylvania and the threat of the French and their Indian allies from Canada. The new settlers were attracted to the region's limestone springs and the treeless prairies, called "barrens." The journal of James McCullough, a Scots-Irish weaver and farmer who moved his family to Conococheague around 1750, noted a variety of crops raised and harvested, including flax and rye (which he wrote as "flex" and "ray"), wheat, buckwheat, oats, turnips, potatoes, hay and other fodder.[4]

The majority of immigrants to the Conococheague settlement were Scots-Irish from Northern Ireland, like McCullough. They were devout Presbyterians and quickly established local congregations. The Scots-Irish never held a strong loyalty to the British government, and their religion set them apart from the Quakers and Anglicans who ran the Pennsylvania government. This contributed to their feelings of alienation when the British army and the government in Philadelphia seemingly failed to protect them adequately when Indians attacked their homes.

In addition to the Scots-Irish in the Conococheague settlement, a lesser number of Welsh established farms along Welsh Run and Germans settled further to the south. They too would play active roles in the Conococheague uprising.

The early years of the Conococheague settlement were peaceful. However, although King George's War (1744-1748) caused no bloodshed in the Mid-Atlantic colonies, the distant threat from the French and their Indian allies created such anxiety that Cumberland Valley inhabitants formed a militia regiment in 1748. Colonel Benjamin Chambers commanded this regiment. Lieutenant William Smith and Major William Maxwell were among its officers.[5]

William Maxwell emigrated from Northern Ireland and, like William Smith, became a prominent figure in the Conococheague settlement. He owned 1,000 acres along the Conococheague's West Branch and near what are now Garnes and Montgomery Church roads. On this tract he built a house called "the Castle" along with grist and clover mills, a distillery, and later a French & Indian War fort. After Cumberland County was established in 1750, William Maxwell became the first justice of peace in the area, and remained so until his death in 1777. Sometimes court was held at his house. In March 1765, at the start of the Conococheague uprising, angry neighbors came to this house twice, blowing up barrels of gunpowder during the second visit. William's bachelor son, James Maxwell, also a magistrate, would side against the uprisers and hear their death threats toward him.[6]

Despite an official peace ending King George's War in 1748, the French aggressively pressed their claim to the Ohio region. The French army, along with Canadian Indians, moved into the Allegheny and Ohio River valleys, building forts, capturing Pennsylvania fur traders and their trade goods, and killing some Miami Indians allied with the British. The French drove off the crew building the fort for the Ohio Company of Virginia at the forks of the Ohio River. This led to 22-year-old Lieutenant Colonel George Washington and his Virginia army company ambushing a French party at Jumonville Glen in May of 1754—the skirmish some claim marked the start of the French & Indian War. French troops subsequently laid siege to Washington and his troops at Fort Necessity, forcing them to surrender on July 4, 1754.

The Ohio Indians had initially resented the French invasion into their home and hunting grounds. At that time, the Iroquois still claimed a tenuous sovereignty over the Delawares and Shawnees who had moved west. The Ohio Iroquois were known as Mingos and their leader was Tanacharison, dubbed the "Half-King" for his role as a viceroy for the Iroquois Six Nations. In April 1754—more than a month before he tomahawked to death French Ensign Joseph Coulon de Jumonville at the glen later named for the French officer—Tanacharison sent messages to the governors of Pennsylvania and Virginia offering to engage the Ohio Delawares, Shawnees, Mingos, and their allies with colonial soldiers and battle the French. However, the defeat of colonial forces at Fort Necessity, dampened the enthusiasm of the Ohio tribes. They wanted to be sure they would be fighting on the winning side, the one that could keep them supplied with presents, ammunition and other trade goods.[7]

News of the Fort Necessity defeat scared frontier inhabitants in Pennsylvania's Cumberland and Lancaster Counties. They sent petitions to Governor James Hamilton[8] asking for arms and protection. Benjamin Chambers topped a list of 75 signers to the Cumberland County petition, dated July 15, 1754. It said:

> . . . we are now in most imminent danger by a powerful army of cruel, merciless and inhumane enemies, by whom our lives, liberties, estates, and all that tends to promote our welfare, are in the utmost danger of dreadful destruction, and this lamentable truth is most evident from the late defeat of the Virginia forces, and now as we are under your Honor's protection, we would beg your immediate notice, we living upon the Frontiers of the Province and our enemies so close upon us, nothing doubting but these considerations will affect your Honor, and as you have our welfare at heart, that you will defer nothing that may tend to hasten our relief . . .[9]

Governor Hamilton could only pass these petitions on to the legislative assembly with his recommendation for them to provide the requested protection. But the assembly was dominated by pacifist Quakers who were loath to supply arms or militia.

Maryland's response was to have its militia build a fort at the confluence of Will's Creek and the North Branch of the Potomac River in 1754. The following year, British General Edward Braddock renamed this Fort Cumberland and used it as a launching point for his expedition to conquer the new French fort, Fort Duquesne, built at the forks of the Ohio (now Pittsburgh). He planned to then move his army northward to Fort Niagara, conquering other French forts on the way.

Braddock assembled more than 2,000 troops at Fort Cumberland, consisting of two British regiments and provincial regular soldiers and militiamen. To reach Fort Duquesne, he slowly built a road through the wilderness sufficient to carry artillery and wagons of supplies to support his marching soldiers.

George Croghan, who had lost most of his trading business due to the French incursion into the Ohio region, acted as an Indian agent during Braddock's campaign. In 1754, Croghan gave sanctuary from the French to

Fort Cumberland, 1755 (Lowdermilk, *History of Cumberland, Md,* 1878)

Tanacharison's and Queen Aliquippa's Mingo people at his Augwick planta-tion settlement (now Shirleysburg, Pennsylvania). The following year he offered their services to Braddock. But Braddock felt the Mingos were poorly equipped and refused all but seven or eight he picked as scouts.

General Braddock had Croghan summon chiefs from the other Ohio tribes. But, according to Shingas, the chief of the Delawares, Braddock haugh-tily rebuked the Indians' demand to keep their land. "No Savage should inherit the Land," he told them. Rather than joining the British or French, the Ohio Delawares and Shawnees generally remained neutral as they waited to see who would win the expected clash at Fort Duquesne. Braddock's failure to employ more Indians is often mentioned as a cause of the disastrous defeat of his army. The Delawares and Shawnees quickly joined the French side afterward. Soon after, Shingas would be called "Shingas the Terrible" by Conococheague and other frontier settlers who experienced the terror of his raids.[10]

Pennsylvania's chief contribution to Braddock's expedition was Benja-min Franklin's valiant effort in procuring needed wagons and horses. Franklin gave his personal bond to farmers, obtaining 259 horses and 150 wagons within two weeks, but found that the new Governor Robert Morris and the legislative assembly could not agree on who should pay for these. The assembly wanted the Penns' proprietary lands taxed along with private lands, but the Penns had made Morris secretly agree to reject any taxes on the proprietary estate. Fortunately for Franklin, as the farmers began to sue him, Massachusetts Governor Shirley became the head of the British army in America and agreed to pay the farmers for their wagons and horses from the army's funds.[11]

When Franklin met Braddock, he felt the general showed "too much self confidence" regarding the threat from Indians. Braddock said: "These sav-ages may be a formidable enemy to your raw American militia, but upon the king's regular and disciplined troops, sir, it is impossible they would make any impression." He was wrong. The Indians would make much more than an im-pression.[12]

To get Pennsylvania's supplies to Braddock's army, a road was commis-sioned in May 1755 to go from the fort at McDowell's Mill on the Conococheague's West Branch to the three forks of the Youghiogheny River, where it would connect with Braddock's own road. Under James Burd, the commissioner of roads, William Smith was charged with oversight of the 300 men building the new road, one of whom was his 18-year-old cousin/brother-in-law. On that road, James Smith became one of the first captives of the French & Indian War.[13]

James Smith was riding with a companion four or five miles from Rays Town (Bedford) when three Indians, a scouting party for the French, shot at them from a blind. They hit and killed Smith's companion, whom they subsequently scalped. They captured Smith when he was thrown from his frightened horse. The Indians took him to Fort Duquesne, where he was beaten while running the gauntlet and then interrogated about the number and strength of men building his road. Smith told them there were 300, but lied in saying they all were armed when few of them were.[14]

General Braddock and about 1,300 to 1,400 soldiers in his vanguard were within fewer than 10 miles from Fort Duquesne on July 9, 1755, when a much smaller force of the French and their Indian allies surprised and attacked them. The subsequent Battle of the Monongahela caused most on the British side to be killed, wounded or captured, while there were remarkably few French and Indian casualties.

With Braddock mortally wounded, the survivors of the devastated British advance guard hastily retreated to the rear while the Indians looted and scalped on the battlefield. James Smith was still a prisoner at Fort Duquesne when Indians returned with booty and prisoners. He later wrote he saw them burn to death British soldiers. Indians eventually took Smith away and a Caughnawaga (Kahnawake) Mohawk tribe adopted him. He lived with them for five years and learned their ways.[15]

Colonel Thomas Dunbar, left in charge of the reserves and rear supplies, took command of the demoralized and disorganized British troops. After burning and destroying his supply wagons and cannon, Dunbar led the retreat to Fort Cumberland. Soon afterward, leaving just the sick and wounded and a few Virginia provincial soldiers at the fort, he marched his army toward Phila-delphia for their winter quarters.[16]

In August 1755, on their way along the Great Valley Road through the Cumberland Valley, Dunbar's troops camped for a while at Pawling's Tavern. This tavern was often called "Pollen's" or similar variations. It was located at the current intersection of Milnor Road and Williamsport Pike just south of Greencastle. The grassy land at Henry Pawling's home and tavern made it a

Braddock's mortal wounding (Mason, *The Romance and Tragedy of Pioneer Life*, 1884)

convenient stopping point for packhorses, wagons, and a defeated army on this occasion. After Henry Pawling died in 1763, the place remained in his family, but was referred to as "John Howe's" or simply "Howe's," perhaps after a new tavern keeper. The names "Howe's" and "Pollen's" were both used during the Conococheague uprising.[17]

As Dunbar and his British troops marched onward to Philadelphia, they left the "back country" inhabitants, including those in the Conococheague settlement, unprotected. When the Pennsylvania government failed to raise funds to supply and keep the British troops in Pennsylvania, Dunbar marched them on to Albany, New York, in October 1755. Cumberland Valley leaders James Burd and John Armstrong asked for help to defend their poorly organized and poorly armed frontier citizens. Without the British army's protection, they were now under an increased threat. Although few, if any, Delawares and Shawnees participated in the French victory on the Monongahela, now their chiefs saw the French as the winning side and joined them against the British colonists.[18]

War served several purposes for the Indians. In addition to gaining power through conquest, achieving revenge or protecting a way of life, war allowed young warriors the opportunity to raise their status through brave deeds and the taking of booty, scalps and captives. The Indians sought captives, particularly women, young men and children, to adopt into families as replacements for loved ones who died through warfare or the white man's diseases like smallpox. The adopted captives were generally well-treated and many later refused to leave their new families. Shingas himself adopted two white boys and treated them as equals to his own children. But those captives who rejected adoption, or did not satisfy the needs of a tribe, could be tortured to death.[19]

The Indian attacks first began to the west and north of the Conococheague settlement. An October 4, 1755 letter to Colonel James Burd at Shippensburg told of 40 whites killed and captured near Fort Cumberland and Patterson Creek, and houses and barns burned. On October 16, 1755, a party of Delawares led by Shingas's brother Pisquetomen attacked the white settlement at Penn's Creek (near today's Selinsgrove, Pennsylvania), killing and scalping

13 adults and an infant, and capturing 11 young men and children. A related group of warriors met with the Delawares living at nearby Shamokin and urged them to join in attacks on the whites.[20]

On November 1, Shingas led a group of about 100 Delawares and Shawnees into the Great Cove settlement, in what is now Fulton County, Pennsylvania. They killed or captured about 50 settlers and burned houses. Of those who survived among the 90 or more families in Great Cove, most fled their homes.[21]

In early November 1755, following reports of the devastation in Great Cove and elsewhere, Governor Morris asked the Pennsylvania assembly to provide arms and ammunition for the frontier. But when the assembly offered him a bill that would pay for these by including taxes on proprietary lands as well as private lands, Morris refused to sign. Benjamin Franklin eventually helped reach a compromise in which the proprietors agreed to pay some of the costs for defense. Franklin pushed through a bill in the assembly to raise voluntary militias and allow them to democratically elect their officers. This was a painful process that left Franklin with contempt for Morris, the Penns, and the pacifist Quakers in the assembly.[22]

The first raid in the Conococheague settlement happened on February 11, 1756, when Indians captured three men or boys along the West Branch of Conococheague Creek, two miles north of McDowell's Mill. On February 29, 1756, after attacking Fort David Davis and other homes in Little Cove, Indians crossed the mountain into the Conococheague valley. As they arrived at the Widow Barr's place (one and a half miles south of the current town of Fort Loudon), a fellow named Alexander discovered them. Alexander ran to alert men in Fort McDowell, the fort at McDowell's Mill on the West Branch of Conococheague Creek, and two miles to the southeast of Widow Barr's.[23]

George Croghan, then a captain in the militia, and 14 men under his command, happened to be at Fort McDowell. The next morning (March 1), Croghan, his men, and 10 or 12 others from the neighborhood, crept up to Widow Barr's and heard the voices of about 50 Indians around a campfire. After getting more reinforcements, Croghan attempted to surround and trap the

Indians. However, somebody fired too soon and most of the Indians escaped. In the melee, the Indians sustained several casualties but killed one white settler and wounded Thomas Barr, the son of Widow Barr.

The Indians who slipped away next attacked Fort McDowell, after shooting dead one of two boys who ran to warn its occupants. Those in the fort held off the attack until Croghan and company heard the shooting and came back. The Indians retreated to Widow Barr's. They placed their dead into a log cabin there and burned it before leaving for the west. A woman who escaped her capture reported that the Indians were warriors under Delaware chiefs Shingas and Captain Jacobs (Tewea), who had told her that they would return in force "when the leaves were out."[24]

The next Conococheague attack was on March 3, 1756 at Heinrich Studebaker's farm at Welsh Run. Indians killed four and captured three Studebaker children.[25]

Fort McCord (northeast of present-day Edenville) was, like Fort McDowell, one of several private forts hurriedly built to protect Conococheague inhabitants. Shingas's warriors secretly observed the activities of that fort for several days and learned that the men left the fort every morning to perform their daily tasks. On April 1, 1756, the Indians attacked the fort when most of its defenders were outside, killed or captured 27 in the fort, and burned down the fort.

The next day, Captain Alexander Culbertson led a party of 51 militia soldiers and caught the Indians and their captives at Sideling Hill (often called Sidelong Hill in colonial times), several miles to the west. In what was a common tactic, the Indians fell back and then surrounded their enemy, killing 21 (including Culbertson) and wounding 17 soldiers. They recaptured their prisoners from Fort McCord, and forced them to watch as they tortured one soldier to death with heated daggers. Another militia group, from Fort Granville on the Juniata River, also pursued the Indians and likewise was defeated.[26]

The frontier inhabitants of Pennsylvania blamed their Quaker-dominated legislative assembly for not providing them with adequate defense against the Indian raids. They held local meetings and resolved to go to Philadelphia to

Indian attack on settlers (Egle, *An Illustrated History of the Commonwealth of Pennsylvania,* 1880)

protest for better defense. According to William Egle: "the dead bodies of some of the murdered and mangled were sent to that city and hauled about the streets, with placards announcing that these were victims of the Quaker policy of non-resistance. A large and threatening mob surrounded the House of Assembly, placed the dead bodies in the doorway, and demanded immediate relief for the people of the frontiers." We can only wonder at the anguish that would cause the people to allow their deceased family members, friends and neighbors to be used in such a manner.[27]

In his council meeting on April 8, 1756 Governor Morris officially declared war against the Delawares and proclaimed rewards for their capture and scalps. The capture of a male above 12 years of age was worth $150. The scalp from a Delaware male, or the capture of a woman or a boy 12 years and under, were each worth $130. A woman's scalp was worth $50. Morris's scalp act forced those Delawares and Shawnees who had still remained neutral to take up arms against the Pennsylvanians.[28]

James McCullough dutifully recorded the deaths and captures of his neighbors in his journal. Like others, his family fled the area (the McCulloughs went to Antietam) but returned periodically to sow and reap crops. On July 26, 1756, McCullough and his family were back at their Conococheague farm to "pull flax" when Indians captured his 8- and 5-year-old sons, John and James. Their father tersely noted their capture in his journal, adding a Biblical quote; "Weep ye not for the dead neither bemoan him but weep sore for him that goeth away for he shall return no more to see his native country."[29]

At Fort Duquesne, a Frenchman took the younger brother, James, and left for Canada. John and the other McCulloughs never saw him again. A Delaware family adopted John, who became well acclimated to Indian life.[30]

John Armstrong of Carlisle, an immigrant from Northern Ireland, was commissioned as a lieutenant colonel in the Pennsylvania provincial army on May 11, 1756. To counterattack the Indian raiders, Armstrong led 300 provincials on a raid of Kittanning, the large Indian village on the Allegheny River in western Pennsylvania from which Shingas and Captain Jacobs launched raids. Three detachments of provincial soldiers left Fort Shirley on August 29 and 30, 1756. The surprise attack on the village began on the morning of September 8. They killed several Indians, including Captain Jacobs, and took some scalps for the bounty. However, the provincials' casualties were high and they managed to rescue fewer than a dozen white captives out of 150 estimated to be there. Most of the Indians fled, taking the bulk of their prisoners with them. If not a great tactical victory, it was a moral one, with the Indians routed and Kittanning partially burned and abandoned.[31]

Despite the destruction of Kittanning and the death of Captain Jacobs, the attacks on the Conococheague settlement continued. Among the raids with greater casualties was one that occurred near Fort McDowell on November 1, 1756, despite the 100 men stationed there to guard and escort "Publick Provisions" westward to other forts. The Indians killed 12 settlers and captured 10. Colonel John Armstrong relayed this sad news in a November 8, 1756 letter to the new Governor William Denny, in which he also noted: "This week, God willing, we will begin the fort at Barr's." Armstrong planned a new provincial fort farther north than McDowell's, nearer to both the road to Carlisle and the mouth of Path Valley. The valley was named for the Indian path through it and along the upper West Branch of Conococheague Creek, which raiders often used.[32]

Armstrong's men found the soil at Widow Barr's place too hard to dig ditches and the site too close to a high hill, so they moved the fort location across the West Branch to Matthew Patton's farm. They eventually named it Fort Loudoun (one of three forts so named; the others being in Virginia and Tennessee) after John Campbell, Fourth Earl of Loudoun, then the British commander-in-chief. By December 22, barracks were ready and the "Publick Stores" moved there from Fort McDowell. At that time, Armstrong recommended that patrols have at least 50 soldiers and two commissioned officers. The fort's stockade was finished later. The number of men garrisoned at Fort Loudoun varied. For example, the fort had 100 men in March 1757, but only 32 in January 1759 and 22 in November 1759.[33]

Fort Loudoun, as one of the forts in the "communication" line westward from Carlisle, served as a supply depot and staging point in both the French & Indian and Pontiac's wars. Although it was never attacked by Indians, it later came under siege from angry local citizenry during the Conococheague uprising in 1765.

Indian attacks on the Conococheague settlement continued in 1757 and through the spring of 1758. During the French & Indian War, the settlement suffered about 40 separate raids. One estimate states that of the 5,000

Re-enactors at Fort Loudoun

people living in the settlement, 233 were killed and 103 captured. Many more fled in terror.[34]

The raids ceased when Brigadier General John Forbes began his expedition toward Fort Duquesne in the summer of 1758. This expedition had more than 6,000 men, consisting of about 2,000 regular British army (mostly Highlanders), with the rest being Pennsylvania and Virginia provincial units. Learning from the mistakes of Braddock, Forbes chose to build a road with intermittent forts along it to protect and supply his troops as they slowly made their way west. To the chagrin of George Washington and other Virginians, Forbes forsook Braddock's Road and chose an all-Pennsylvania route with better forage areas and smaller rivers to cross. The first part of this road, "Forbes Road," was along the road originally cut by James Burd and William Smith.[35]

General Forbes was sick and dying during the expedition, and relied heavily on his Swiss-born second-in-command, Colonel Henry Bouquet, to direct road, fort, and depot construction, and the movement of the troops and supplies. Colonel John Armstrong's 1st Battalion of Cumberland Valley provincials joined into Forbes' troops. The forts Armstrong defended served as camps and supply depots. From Carlisle, the expedition moved on to Fort Loudoun, and then passed Forts Lyttleton, Bedford, and Ligonier, on its way to the forks of the Ohio.[36]

As Forbes' troops neared Fort Duquesne in September 1758, Major James Grant of the 77th Regiment of Foot (Montgomery's Scottish Highlanders) was ordered to undertake a reconnaissance mission with 800 men to determine the French strength at Fort Duquesne. Grant bungled this assignment by attempting to capture the fort instead. Indians and French soldiers ambushed and routed his troops, causing hundreds of casualties. Major Grant and an 18-year-old relative, Charles Grant, were among those captured. The Wyandots held Charles, a "volunteer" in the 77th Regiment, prisoner until 1760. After his release, Charles Grant rejoined the army, was promoted to lieutenant, and became a nemesis and target of the 1765 Conococheague uprising.

Following a failed attempt to take Fort Ligonier and with supplies running out, the French and their remaining Indian allies decided to flee rather than fight when the main body of Forbes' expedition came within a few miles of Fort Duquense. The British found the fort abandoned and blown up when they entered it on November 24 or 25, 1758. General Forbes only briefly visited the fort's ruins and died of his illness shortly afterwards. The British built and manned a new fort, named Fort Pitt, at the confluence of the Allegheny and Monongahela Rivers.[37]

Before the fall of Fort Duquense, Moravian missionary Christian Frederick Post and Delaware chief Pisquetomen had been negotiating for peace with both the Ohio Indians and the Pennsylvania government. This helped set up the Treaty of Easton, signed in October 1758. The Delawares and Shawnees agreed to leave the side of the French. In return, Governor William Denny agreed to the natives' right to the lands west of the Allegheny Mountains. George Croghan participated in the treaty. Afterward, Croghan and 15 Indian warriors he recruited there joined the Forbes' expedition on November 20.[38]

The Treaty of Easton and Forbes' conquest of Fort Duquesne in late 1758 essentially ended the French & Indian War in Pennsylvania. However, the war continued in the north and worldwide—as part of the global Seven Years' War.

In the Conococheague settlement and elsewhere on the Pennsylvania frontier, families returned and built new houses and barns to replace those the Indians had burned. The loss of loved ones and neighbors, and memories of the recent terror must have made resuming life to what it was before very hard, if not impossible, for many. One issue that grated was learning about captives still alive and living with the Ohio Indians, and who were not being sent home.

Moravian missionaries making peace
(Mason, *The Romance and Tragedy of Pioneer Life,* 1884)

James McCullough learned the whereabouts of his son John from a trader in 1760, and went west twice in attempts to pay ransom and recover the boy from captivity. On the second try, in 1762, James got his son but John resisted his return, escaped, and eventually went back to his Delaware family. Not until 1764, as part of their negotiations at the end of Pontiac's War, did the Ohio Indians gave up all their captives. Only then did John McCullough return to his Conococheague family after living eight years with the Ohio Delawares. He later wrote a long narrative of his life with the Indians, which described their customs in detail.[39]

One captive who returned earlier to the Conococheague was James Smith. In 1759, Smith traveled with Indian companions to the Mohawk town of Caughnawaga, where he left them and went nine miles farther into Montreal. The French imprisoned him in Montreal for four months and then freed him in an exchange for other prisoners at Crown Point, New York. He walked back to the Conococheague settlement and, to the delighted surprise of his family, ended his five-year absence.[40]

The retreat of the French army from the Ohio region, followed by the fall of Fort Niagara in July 1759, eliminated the French supply line for ammunition and other European goods to the Ohio Indians. The Indians were thus desperate to resume trade with the British colonies. But the few traders who initially went west were unlicensed and sold substandard goods at high prices. The Indians complained. To keep the peace, the Quaker Friendly Association spent over 3,000 pounds on gifts, which they distributed to the Indians at Fort Pitt. But a continuing access to European supplies and ammunition through trade would remain a critical need to the Ohio Delawares, Shawnees and Mingos.[41]

General John Stanwix took command in the west following Forbes's death. He sent George Croghan to Fort Pitt in June 1759 to confirm peace with the Ohio Indians, and to invite them to a conference in Philadelphia that summer. Through meetings at different Ohio villages, Croghan learned that the Indians remained suspicious of British intentions and thus would not go to the conference. He also learned of their reluctance to return captives they had adopted into their tribes. Tamaqua ("the Beaver"), who replaced his brother Shingas as head of the Delawares, turned over two white women that he had adopted into his own family. But the others refused to follow his example.[42]

Chapter 2

Indians Attack Again
Pontiac's War

Fighting in the French & Indian War ceased for all North America after the French surrendered Canada in September 1760. The signing of the Treaty of Paris on February 10, 1763 formally ended this war, as well as the global Seven Years' War. To the chagrin of Indians throughout eastern North America, and the Ohio Indians in particular, the treaty gave Great Britain the land they felt belonged to them, not the French. Additionally, the British increased the number of troops in the forts they built or captured from the French rather than withdrawing them as promised. The Indians feared that the British intended to eliminate them.[43]

During this time, Sir Jeffery Amherst—commander-in-chief of the British army in North America since September 1758—implemented a strict Indian policy. Amherst forbade giving presents to Indians, partly to lower the expense of military operations (the French & Indian War had cost Great Britain dearly) and partly due to his own low regard for Native Americans. He also directed that ammunition not be given to or traded with Indians, disregarding that the Indians needed ammunition for hunting as well as warfare. Sir William Johnson, George Croghan, and commanding officers at outposts warned him that this would cause future problems, but Amherst saw the Indians as a conquered people who "must be punished and not bribed." Like Braddock before

Sir Jeffery Amherst by Sir Joshua Reynolds

him, Amherst underestimated the threat of their discontent. The Indians felt that although the French had been beaten by the British, they had not been. They wanted trade and present-giving to continue as before.[44]

Although anger brewed among the Indians, the Conococheague settlement remained at peace in early 1763. James Smith married Ann Wilson. Tradition says they settled just south of Widow Barr's place, on a hill near the present Mountain View Elementary School on Pa. Route 75. James and Ann eventually had four sons and three daughters.[45]

When the Ottawa chief Pontiac attacked Fort Detroit in May 1763, it sparked a general native uprising that spread along the Great Lakes and into the Illinois and Ohio regions. Forts Detroit and Niagara withstood attacks, but eight other forts along the Great Lakes and in northwest Pennsylvania fell to Indians.

24

The Ohio Indians remembered their raids on the Pennsylvania and Virginia frontiers from 1755 to 1758 as successes, and that experience gave them confidence to attack there again. They hoped to drive the British from their forts, protect their dominion over the land, and steal what European supplies they could. In July 1763, Ohio Delawares, Shawnees and Mingos attacked at Forts Pitt, Ligonier and Bedford. The garrisons posted at those forts held firm but the Indians killed and captured settlers nearby the forts. Soon after, they moved farther east and attacked farms and plantations along the Juniata River, the Tuscarora and Sherman Valleys, and along the foot of North Mountain—areas to the west and north of Carlisle and Shippensburg.[46]

Remembering the terror of a few years prior, thousands fled to the middle part of Cumberland County. The *Pennsylvania Gazette* reported:

> Flying families, obliged to abandon House and Possession, to save their Lives by an hasty Escape; mourning Widows, bewailing their Husbands surprized and massacred by savage Rage; tender Parents, lamenting the Fruit of their own Bodies, cropt in the very Bloom of Life by a barbarous Hand; with Relations and Acquaintances, pouring out Sorrow for murdered Neighbours and Friends, present a varied Scene of mingled Distress.[47]

Churches and charities in Philadelphia and Lancaster provided financial aid to the displaced families.

The British army responded to Pontiac's War by first supplying and re-manning the forts that withstood Indian sieges, and later by sending expeditions into Indian territories. General Thomas Gage replaced Sir Jeffery Amherst as the commander-in-chief in North America. In Pennsylvania, Colonel Henry Bouquet's expedition to resupply Fort Pitt and other forts along Forbes Road clashed with Indians at the Battle of Bushy Run on August 5 and 6, 1763. Feigning a retreat to draw out and trap the Indians, Bouquet turned a potential defeat into a victory and went on to relieve Fort Pitt. Afterward, Indians temporarily disappeared from all of Cumberland County.

Colonel Henry Bouquet (left) & General Thomas Gage (right)

The Pennsylvania government's response to attacks on the frontier was to raise provincial troops and to pass a law forbidding the arming of the attackers. Governor James Hamilton approved "An Act to prohibit the selling of Guns, Powder, or other Warlike Stores to the Indians" on October 22, 1763. This act was still in affect in early 1765, when Conococheague inhabitants embraced it as part of their justification for actions against traders and British troops.[48]

The Royal Proclamation of 1763 had been issued earlier that month, on October 7. It forbade whites from settling west of the Allegheny Mountain, as the Treaty of Easton had done previously. Many hoped in vain that this restriction on settlement would appease the Indians. The proclamation also would have opened up trade with Indians, with the caveat that traders be licensed. It said:

> the Trade with the said Indians shall be free and open to all our Subjects whatever, provided that every Person who may incline to Trade with the said Indians do take out a Licence for carrying on such Trade from the Governor or Commander in Chief of any of our Colonies respectively where such Person shall reside, and also give Security to observe such Regulations as We shall at any Time think fit, by ourselves

or by our Commissaries to be appointed for this Purpose, to direct and appoint for the Benefit of the said Trade.[49]

Despite James Smith's statement and those of others since that "the king's proclamation prohibited trade," the banning of Indian trade really came from the governor's control of licenses and the Pennsylvania (and similar New Jersey) law forbidding the sale of "warlike stores." It is telling that when General Gage later wanted to reopen trade with the Ohio Indians, he asked the new Governor John Penn to do so, and Penn had the power to refuse his request and initially did.[50]

The newspapers reported no attacks in the Conococheague settlement in 1763. The survival of all the forts on Forbes Road—from Fort Pitt to Fort Loudoun—likely provided some deterrence to the Ohio Indians raiding so far that year. But credit is more likely due to warnings and protection from scouting patrols or rangers led by John Armstrong, Captain Shelby and James Smith.

James Smith, as a former Indian captive, taught his rangers to adopt an Indian style in dress and tactics. He wrote of how the locals:

Pennsylvania Governors James Hamilton (left) and John Penn (right)

. . . raised as much money by collections and subscriptions, as would pay a company of rifle-men for several months. The subscribers met and elected a committee to manage the business. The committee appointed me captain of this company of rangers, and gave me the appointment of my subalterns. I chose two of the most active young men that I could find, who had also been long in captivity with the Indians. As we enlisted our men, we dressed them uniformly in the Indian manner with breech-clouts, leggins, mockesons and green shrouds, which we wore in the same manner that the Indians do, and nearly as the Highlanders wear their plaids. In place of hats we wore red handkerchiefs, and painted our faces red and black, like Indian warriors. I taught them the Indian discipline, as I knew of no other at that time, which would answer the purpose much better than British. We succeeded beyond expectation in defending the frontiers, and were extolled by our employers.[51]

By September 1763, those "employers" were running out of funds so they petitioned the Pennsylvania assembly to take over support of the rangers. On September 17, the following "Petition from the Inhabitants of the Great Cove, and Conecocheague, in the County of Cumberland" was read to the assembly members:

. . . the Petitioners, by the late Depredations and Ravages of the Indians committed on their Neighbours, being in very imminent Danger, were under the Necessity of taking into Pay a Number of Men, amounting to about Thirty, accustomed to hunting, enured to Hardship, and well acquainted with the Country, for the Protection of themselves and Families: That the said Men (being a Body of intrepid, resolute Fellows, under the Command of one who was a Captive with the Indians for several Years) scouted at a considerable Distance, and, by dispatching Runners, gave the Inhabitants timely Notice of any impending Danger, by Means whereof they have been enabled to continue on their Plantations, and stand a Barrier to the interior neighbouring Settlements: That had not this Expedient been fallen upon, they must have deserted their Habitations, and depended upon the Charities of others; and that although they are very sensible of, and gratefully acknowledge, the Care of the Legislature, in granting a Number of Men for the Protection of the Frontiers, yet they find themselves under the Necessity of employing this Body of Men, inasmuch as the Soldiers granted for their Department are not acquainted with the Country, or the Indian Manner of fighting: That the Petitioners are poor, and incapable of supporting this Body of Men, having already advanced greater Sums than they could afford; and unless they are assisted by the Government, shall be obliged to abandon their Plantations to the Savages, to the Ruin of themselves, and great Injury of their Neighbours: For which Reasons they humbly pray the House would take the Premises into Consideration, and enable them to continue the aforesaid Body of Men, in such Manner, and subject to such Directions, as they shall judge most proper and advantageous.[52]

The former captive and leader of the rangers cited in the petition must have been James Smith's second-in-command, not Smith himself. Smith had resigned from the rangers before July 16, 1763, the day he received an ensign's commission in Colonel John Armstrong's provincial regiment. Smith wrote: "upon my resignation, my lieutenant succeeded me in command."[53]

The provincial assembly initially tabled the petition, then read it again, and "after some debate, unanimously rejected" it. Without funds, the Conococheague rangers, those "intrepid, resolute Fellows," soon disbanded. Undoubtedly the central government's refusal of the Conococheague settlers' plea to support the group they saw as having successfully protected them, coupled with the violence they experienced the next year, further alienated the settlers.

Colonel Armstrong's Cumberland County regiment was not yet fully formed during Colonel Bouquet's 1763 expedition to Fort Pitt and did not join in. Instead it stayed for a while in Carlisle as a home guard, patrolling the region. In the fall of 1763, Armstrong gathered his troops and campaigned to the north on the West Branch of the Susquehanna River, with the intent of raiding the Indians on Great Island. They found only villages abandoned by the retreating Delawares and Munsees, which Armstong's men burned along with the Indian cornfields and stores of corn.[54]

Indians temporarily disappeared from all of Cumberland County after Colonel Henry Bouquet's troops defeated the Indians at Bushy Run and resupplied Fort Pitt and its "line of communication" that is, the Forbes Road forts. One writer from Carlisle happily declared in January 1764 that "our Frontier now rests in Peace." However, peace did not last.[55]

In December 1763, violence occurred to the east, in Lancaster County. But there the victims were Conestoga Indians and the perpetrators were a Scots-Irish vigilante group known since as the "Paxton Boys." The Conestogas were peaceful and relied on subsidies from the provincial government. Such charity was resented by the Scots-Irish, who felt that their own defense was not being adequately funded by the government in Philadelphia. The "Boys" claimed that the Conestogas, and particularly one called Will Sock, had aided hostile Indians. Fifty-seven Paxton Boys raided the Conestoga village on December 14, burning cabins and killing the only six Indians they found.[56]

On December 27, 50 Paxton Boys killed and scalped six adult Conestogas (including Will Sock and his wife) and eight children who had been placed in protective custody in a Lancaster workhouse. Despite a reward offered by the provincial government, the attackers were never identified and tried.

In January 1764, the Paxton Boys' ranks grew to several hundred as they marched toward Philadelphia to attack other peaceful Indians protected and subsidized there, and to protest their dissatisfaction with the poor protection the Pennsylvania government had given them against past Indian attacks. Philadelphians were terrified. Benjamin Franklin and other civic leaders met the mob at Germantown, heard their grievances, and persuaded the mob to disperse. Governor Penn met secretly with the Paxton Boys and, in an attempt to win favor with the Presbyterian frontiersmen, he agreed not to press charges against them.[57]

Philadelphians panicked by the approach of the Paxton Boys
(Mason, *The Romance and Tragedy of Pioneer Life*, 1884)

Penn's failure to prosecute the Paxton Boys and other moves he made to align himself with Presbyterians and Germans further rankled Ben Franklin and the Quaker-dominated assembly. Franklin published his *Narrative of the Late Massacres*, which attacked the Paxton Boys, Presbyterianism, and the Penn family. According to historian Kevin Kenny, this "triggered a pamphlet war in 1764, that culminated in his [Franklin's] ill-conceived proposal for a royal government in Pennsylvania."[58]

John Armstrong insisted to Governor Penn no one in Cumberland County was involved with the Conestoga massacres. However, the provincial government and the British army clearly recalled the rebellious nature of Scots-Irish frontiersmen when the Conococheague uprising began a year later.[59]

In its January 10, 1764 session, the provincial assembly heard two petitions pleading for defensive measures in Cumberland County. One "from a Number of Inhabitants" asked that troops continue to be stationed on the frontiers of the county, and "with such Additions" the assembly might think proper for defense. The second, from David Scott in Great Cove, was similar to the September 17, 1763 "Petition from the Inhabitants of the Great Cove, and Conecocheague, in the County of Cumberland." Scott praised the effectiveness of a scouting party of 27 men "who could shoot with great Exactness, and were well acquainted with the Woods, and the Indian Manner of Fighting, some of them having been long in Captivity." He said the Indians stayed out of Great Cove when this party was privately paid and active. But when he and his neighbors no longer could fund them and they disbanded, the Indians "butchered and carried into Captivity some of the Settlers." Scott begged the assembly to fund this party. However, the assembly tabled both petitions.[60]

In its March 23, 1764 session, the assembly considered a petition signed by 1,200 inhabitants of Cumberland County. They asked for six things: (1) a circuit court in the county, (2) compensation for inhabitants who suffered losses from Indian attacks and an end to "public money" being given to Indians ("pretended Friends"), (3) the end of all trade with Indians until all white captives were returned, (4) remuneration and medical care for volunteers who marched against the enemy Indians, (5) rejection of proposals in the assembly they felt would deprive the counties "of the Rights of British Subjects," and (6) an increase in representation in the assembly. Some of these requests were met later, such as the eventual release of the captives and the establishment of a circuit court (in 1767).[61]

In April 1764, General Thomas Gage sent orders to Colonel John Bradstreet and Colonel Henry Bouquet directing their preparation for summer expeditions into Indian country. Bradstreet was to sail his troops across Lake Erie, reinforce Fort Detroit, and march into the Ohio region from the north. Bouquet was to lead his troops to Fort Pitt and then into the Ohio region from the east. Both expeditions were delayed over problems in recruiting colonial men. By the end of May, Bouquet was already complaining of how desertion depleted the ranks of provincial troops and suggested to Gage that offering pardons to deserters who rejoined might be a solution.[62]

Bouquet used Fort Loudoun as a staging area and supply depot for his Ohio expedition. Captain Robert Callender served as his supplier of the vast amount of food needed. Callender was a former trader and associate of George Croghan, repaired Forbes Road in 1758, and served as second-in-command under John Armstrong in 1763. On March 27, 1764, he wrote to Bouquet about the status of flour and also the general fear of impending attacks at Fort Loudoun and nearby:

> There is now about two thousand small Casks of Flour at Fort Loudon, & about six hundred at M. Dowell's Mill, & not one Soldier there, or scarce any at Loudon, as the few that remains are always out on the Scout; So that if any strong party of Indians shoud come down, there wou'd Certainly be a great [risk] in keeping so much flour there unguarded. People in general Seems to be more affrighted now, than at any thing of the kind that ever yet happned; they who never left their habitations before, are now flying in the greatest precipitation to places of Refuge. People is now begining to dispare of getting in any Spring Crop. When I was up, Mr McDowell & Several others were desiring me to apply to You, to see if you wou'd order the Regulars to Loudon, which woud be the means of keeping hundreds on their Places, but I told at the same time it woud be taking too much upon me to Ask for the like. We are also Extreamly ill of for want of stores at that place, & is always distressd in gitting any party of.[63]

In the Conococheague settlement, inhabitants heard about the resumption of Indian raids to the north and west of them in the spring of 1764. In June, after a hiatus of six years, Indians struck their homes again. On June 1, a man tending his cattle at the Armstrong plantation—a half-mile from Fort Loudoun—was shot through his arm. The next day, six miles "below" the fort, Indians killed and scalped a man and then captured his wife and four small children. Parties from the fort tracked the raiders but lost them. And on June 4, a man was found dead and scalped on the road from Fort Loudoun to Shippensburg.[64]

A June 5, 1764 Indian raid caused the greatest death toll in the Conococheague settlement that year with 19 or 20 killed. Four miles downstream of Fort Loudoun, along the West Branch of Conococheague Creek, 13 people within three families were murdered and their homes burned. The Indians captured seven or eight others. One boy escaped and reported there were 20 raiders. As troops from the fort and local inhabitants pursued the Indians, they killed all their remaining captives and then scattered and escaped.[65]

On July 7, 1764, Governor John Penn reinstated bounties for Indian captures and scalps. He had already promised to do so in his secret meeting with the Paxton Boys and now other Presbyterian frontiersmen were under attack. His proclamation clarified that the Delawares, Shawnees and others who were attacking the frontier were their enemies and subject to the bounties, while the Six Nations of the Iroquois and any Indians under the Pennsylvania government's protection were not. The latter clause was obviously in response to the Paxton Boys' massacres.[66]

The rewards and age limits in the 1764 bounties were slightly different from those in 1756. The capture of a male Indian enemy older than 10 would be rewarded by 150 Spanish dollars, or pieces of eight. Their scalps would yield 134 pieces of eight. For younger males and all females the reward for capture would be 130 pieces of eight. The scalps of female Indians older than 10 would be 50 pieces of eight. (Apparently there was no bounty on children's scalps.) Soldiers in the pay of the province would be rewarded bounties at half these rates.[67]

Partly for revenge and partly to get the new bounties, Ensign James Smith and seven others formed a scalping party that traveled 70 miles down the Ohio River from Fort Pitt. They found only deserted villages, a few tracks, and just a single Indian.[68]

John McCullough recalled that while in captivity during the summer of 1764, 300 or more Indians gathered at the forks of the Muskingum River in the Ohio region. They debated whether to invade the Pennsylvania frontier as one large group and massacre settlers. After holding a council for 10 days, they decided that their own towns would be undefended if they all went together, so instead smaller groups left "for different parts of the settlement."[69]

On July 25, Susan Cunningham was going from her house to Justice McDowell's house, two miles from Fort Loudoun, when Indians brutally killed and scalped her, and cut out her unborn child. The raiders also captured a woman named Jamieson that day.[70]

The next day, July 26, 1764, three or four Delawares conducted one of the most notorious of Indian attacks. At a schoolhouse located between present-day Williamson and Greencastle, the Indians shot and killed the schoolmaster—Enoch Brown—and then tomahawked and scalped his students. The number of child casualties varies with different accounts, but 10 dead with one surviving his scalping now seems to be the most commonly stated. The massacre of so many children was particularly repulsive, even to the elders of the Delawares.[71]

Monument and grave marker at Enoch Brown School massacre site

The captive John McCullough was well acquainted with three Indians, "none more than twenty" years old, who massacred Enoch Brown and his students. When those young raiders returned to Ohio and showed off their scalps, the "old Indians" expressed their displeasure with the "cowardice" of killing so many children.[72]

Both General Gage and Colonel Bouquet observed that, despite's Amherst's policy, initially the Ohio Indians appeared to be "well supplied with ammunition." Bouquet speculated that the likely source was Fort de Chartres on the east bank of the Mississippi River in present-day Illinois. Although the stone fort had been officially ceded to the British by the Treaty of Paris in 1763, French settlers and traders who received supplies up the Mississippi from New Orleans still remained there. The British army did not occupy that fort and force out the French until October 1765.[73]

Colonel Henry Bouquet arrived in Carlisle from Philadelphia in early August 1764. There he advertised for volunteers for his Ohio expedition, appealing to men to "serve their country." He noted that while it was "not in my Power" to pay the volunteers, they could partake in the bounties for Indian captives and scalps. When Bouquet and his troops marched west in large convoys later that month, he left behind his deputy quartermaster general at Fort Loudoun and stationed 50 men each at Forts Loudoun, Bedford and Ligonier in order to escort smaller supply convoys to Fort Pitt on a monthly basis. However, while at Fort Loudoun, Bouquet wrote of his displeasure with its condition:[74]

> The Store houses for Provisions at this Fort are in ruinous Condition, having orginaly been only little huts of Logs for Provincial Soldiers, and Swarming with Rats, by which the Provisions suffer considerably. The Place belongs to a Farmer [Matthew Patton], and is inconvenient in Every Respect.[75]

Colonel Bouquet suffered the desertion of many troops, particularly from the provincials. Governor Penn issued an appeal to the two Pennsylvania battalions to obey their enlistment oaths and not forget their duty to "King and Country." He also ordered the magistrates to apprehend deserters and those who assisted and harbored them. But by mid-August, of the 950 men promised for Pennsylvania provincials, 200 had deserted, taking arms and horses with them. This undoubtedly created tensions between the British army and local settlers. To replace the Pennsylvanian deserters, Colonel Bouquet requested 200 Virginia volunteer riflemen who joined him at Fort Pitt. Later, those Virginians left Bouquet in anger when he failed to pay them. Next March, when the Black Boys attacked a packhorse train and destroyed its goods, they tried to shift the blame to "the Virginians."[76]

As Bouquet assembled and marched his army from Carlisle and Fort Loudoun, Indians were spotted nearly every day in the Conococheague settlement. They were spying on Bouquet's maneuvers. On August 9, four Indians chased two settlers near Justice McDowell's place (near the present day village of Markes). Those were the last Indian warriors reported in the Conococheague area. Sightings of Indians occurred in other parts of Cumberland County through the end of August, but in mid-September a report stated: "All appears quiet at present along the Frontier, except about Bedford . . ."[77]

In October 1764, Bouquet camped his army on the Muskingum River in the Ohio country and negotiated with the Delawares who lived there, the Mingos, and the Shawnees who traveled east from their principal towns on the Scioto River. James Smith, now promoted to lieutenant, was there with Armstrong's provincial battalion and served as an interpreter. Lieutenant Charles Grant was also on the Muskingum, with his 42nd Royal Highland Regiment of Foot, known as the "Black Watch."[78]

By then, the Ohio Indians were low on ammunition and thus less of a threat. Key issues in the negotiations were the release of white captives, the resumption of trade, and the continuation of the promise not to settle on Indian lands. The Indians agreed to return their captives, including those adopted into families during the French & Indian War and any new children born to white women. Bouquet received and marched "upwards of 200 Captives" from Muskingum to Fort Pitt, and the Shawnees returned others to the fort in May

Indians Delivering English Captives to Colonel Bouquet by Benjamin West

1765. Bouquet's bloodless expedition is credited with releasing 278 white captives, many (if not most) of whom had become "white Indians" and needed to be guarded to prevent their escape back to their Indian families.[79]

James Smith credited Bouquet's success in Ohio to his having the troops march and camp in a scattered pattern, as the Indians did: "After we left Fort Pitt, we marched on the oblong square, with flankers, and encamped on the hollow square." At Muskingum, Smith met with Indians he had once lived with and they told him: "if the red coats had come as usual in close order, they could have readily subdued them."[80]

Smith was suspicious of the peace. His interpretation of the treaty was that warfare would cease for six months, until all the white captives were returned. The Indians appointed hostages to be held at Fort Pitt until they met the negotiated conditions. But Smith noted that six Shawnee hostages escaped and some Indians "stole horses and killed some people on the frontiers." James Smith and others on the frontier remained wary of the Ohio Indians.[81]

Colonel Bouquet was afraid that it would be the whites who would break the fragile peace. Members of the Maryland militia killed and scalped an Indian at Pittsburg. Bouquet heard of others "in the woods" with similar purposes: "The Licenciousness of the Frontier Inhabitants in general is carried to a high degree, and unless Severe Measures are taken to restrain them within proper Bounds, and Hunting beyond the Allegheny Mountains is expressly forbid to them, It will be impossible to preserve Peace with the Indians."[82]

However, Bouquet's 1764 Ohio expedition and his negotiations with the Indians brought about a great decrease in the violence on the frontier. A report from Fort Pitt noted that "the Post enjoyed a perfect Calm, not an Indian being to be seen on the Communication, by which People with Loads of Butter, Cheese, &c. arrived there daily unmolested." A Carlisle report stated "all is very quiet there; our People, in general, returning to their Places."[83]

Indian attacks on the Conococheague settlement ended before the fall of 1764. Colonel Henry Bouquet personally enjoyed the peace on the Conococheague around Christmas that year. His letters dated December 20 and 22, 1764 at "Conegocheague" imply that on his way back to Philadelphia, he visited the home he purchased in the settlement in 1763. That was the former Long Meadows plantation once owned by Thomas Cresap, and located north of present-day Hagerstown, Maryland. Had he lived so long, the Swiss-born Bouquet might have settled at his Conococheague home.[84]

The total of Conococheague settler casualties cited in 1764 newspaper accounts were 34 killed, two wounded and six captured. Unreported events may have made the actual totals higher, but they would have been nowhere near as great as those for the 1756-1758 period. Nevertheless, the violence and terror of 1764 were fresh in memory of James Smith and his "Black Boys" the next year. Their anger toward traders attempting to re-arm the Indians in violation of Pennsylvania's law, with the aid and protection of British troops at Fort Loudoun, would be the cause of the Conococheague uprising of 1765.

Although the Penns and their governors balked at proposed defensive measures that would tax the proprietors' lands, Cumberland County inhabitants instead generally blamed the Quakers in the assembly for the poor defense of their frontier. In the fall of 1764, Cumberland County voters elected assemblymen on the proprietor's side—John Montgomery and William Allen. Allen was the head of the proprietary faction, and well connected as the father-in-law of Governor John Penn. He also served as the Chief Justice of Pennsylvania from 1751 through 1774. The fact that William Allen lived in Philadelphia was not a deterrent to Cumberland County voters; he remained their assemblyman until a 1770 law made such absentee representation illegal.[85]

Bouquet's and Bradstreet's 1764 expeditions brought a temporary peace to the Pennsylvania, Maryland and Virginia frontiers. Bouquet told the Ohio Indians that trade would resume when they reached a formal treaty with Sir William Johnson, head of Indian affairs under the British commanding general. (That treaty was not concluded until the spring of the next year.) And the British still needed to make peace with the Illinois Indians and with Pontiac himself. General Gage decided that the latter objectives would be better reached through diplomacy rather than conquest, particularly given orders from England to keep military costs low. Learning from Amherst's mistakes and with council from Johnson and George Croghan, Gage knew that diplomacy required presents for the Indians and that trade with the Indians should resume as soon as reasonable.[86]

In December 1764, Gage wrote to Governor Penn encouraging him "to give such notice as you see convenient, to the Merchants, that the Trade may be carried on with the several Nations" (the Ohio tribes). However, as with James Smith, the escape of the Shawnee hostages gave the governor's council unease about the peace brokered by Bouquet. They advised the governor to wait until the formal peace agreement was made with Sir William Johnson. Penn agreed and thus the ban on trade remained in effect during the first half of 1765.[87]

Like George Croghan, William Johnson had immigrated from Ireland, traded and associated with Indians (particularly the Mohawks near his New

York home), and served in the colonial troops. In 1756, as the superintendent of Indian affairs, Johnson appointed Croghan, a Pennsylvanian, to be his deputy with an annual salary of £200. In that position, which he held for 15 years, Croghan was not supposed to trade with or buy and sell land from the Indians. But he did so in secret. Croghan's biographer, Nicholas B. Wainwright, applauded his abilities and many successes in Indian diplomacy, but noted "Croghan did not keep his promises; he was not candid; he misrepresented; he lied."[88]

In 1763, Croghan established a clandestine business connection with the Philadelphia merchant firm of Baynton, Wharton and Morgan. He sold them western lands and promised to buy trade goods from them. Next Croghan took a sabbatical from his Indian agent duties and sailed to England. There he requested reparations from the Board of Trade to reimburse for goods that traders like he and merchants like Baynton, Wharton and Morgan had lost in 1754 and 1763, respectively at the start of the French & Indian and Pontiac's wars. The Board failed to respond in favor of the merchants and traders.[89]

Back in Philadelphia in November 1764, George Croghan secretly joined a partnership with Baynton, Wharton and Morgan, Robert Field and Robert Callender to provide £20,000 worth of trade goods to the western Indians. Croghan held a 25 percent interest in this venture. Their ambition was to be the first British merchants in the beaver trade with the Illinois Indians. But the war with those Indians needed to end first.[90]

John Baynton and Samuel Wharton ran a long-standing mercantile firm in Philadelphia, which took on George Morgan as a partner. George Croghan and Robert Callender were fur-trading partners in 1752 and likely even before that. Callender's letters were often marked as being written at Pennsborough, near Carlisle, Pennsylvania. Croghan operated out of his Pennsborough plantation on Conodoguinet Creek from 1745 to 1751, after which he moved over the mountains to Aughwick Creek.[91]

From Philadelphia, George Croghan traveled to New York to see General Gage. Croghan and others convinced Gage that he, Croghan, was the man to negotiate peace with the Illinois Indians. Gage gave Croghan a credit of

£2,000 to buy Indian presents. In Philadelphia again, Croghan bought much more than that limit allowed. Using his cousin Thomas Smallman (just released by the Shawnees after a year and a half of captivity) as his proxy, Croghan bought goods for trading as well as for giving away as Crown presents. Pretending all were presents, he had Colonel Henry Bouquet write passes to take the goods to Fort Pitt.[92]

Bouquet also wrote to the post commanders on January 12, 1765, directing them to:

> give to George Croghan Esq[r] D. Agent for Indian Affairs, all the assistance he may Stand in need of, on his Way to and From the Ohio, and They are to permit the Ammunition, Dry Goods and Liquors, which he is take with him as presents to the Indians to pass unmolested along the Communication, upon his Certificates Specifying the Number of horses employed, the different Sorts of Goods carried, and that they are for his Majesty's use, and Every Officer will keep Copys of this order and of the several Certificates to justify the Passage of the Said Presents.[93]

Colonel Bouquet's orders thus required some bookkeeping by the post commanders, to document the type and amount of goods Croghan and his cohorts were transporting.

George Croghan most likely used wagons to take the initial shipment of his goods to Carlisle, where he hired 65 packhorses to carry the goods farther. In late February or early March 1765, Croghan, his packhorse train, and Lieutenant Alexander Fraser reached Fort Pitt.[94]

Croghan and his partners had many more Indian goods to move to Fort Pitt in anticipation of when trade would be resumed. When later caught secretly transporting these goods before trade had reopened, the guilty parties so muddied the truth that it is still impossible to know what exactly were Crown presents and what were illegal trade goods.

Robert Callender was in charge of the next shipments to be sent to Fort Pitt. According to his own deposition for a grand jury, he was managing £15,000 worth of goods shipped from Philadelphia in about 20 wagons in the months of January and February 1765. These went to "a house of his . . . within ten miles" of Carlisle, presumably in Pennsborough. From there Callender sent "light loads" of goods in 16 or 17 wagons to "the house of John Howe in Antrim township" (that is, to Pawling's Tavern). From the difference in wagon counts, a portion of the goods must have stayed at Callender's house. Callender said that at Howe's he hired a number of horses and packhorse men to take the goods from there to Fort Pitt. Magistrate James Maxwell later testified that Callender contracted with "Henry Prater" (Prather) for 200 packhorses. Robert Allison testified that he and others were contracted to deliver the goods to Fort Pitt at the rate of three pounds and ten shillings for each horse load.[95]

James Maxwell, in his grand jury deposition, said that on December 23 or 24, 1764, Robert Callender told him of his plans to store goods in the Conococheague area. Later Maxwell learned that Callender sent his clerk, John Irwin, to Fort Loudoun to "procure storage for these goods" there, but found it

Site of Pawling's Tavern (Howe's), south of Greencastle

unsuitable and thus chose Howe's (Pawling's Tavern) for storage. Perhaps Irwin's choice was made after finding rats and other poor conditions at Fort Loudoun as Colonel Bouquet had noted the summer before. Or perhaps Callender really wanted to avoid Fort Loudoun because of the certificate-checking and related bookkeeping that Colonel Bouquet's letter to post commanders ordered—producing documents that would record more goods than needed for Indian presents passing through to Fort Pitt. In any case, Maxwell's testimony tells us he was an early confidant of Robert Callender. As a magistrate, James Maxwell would take the side of the traders and troops while other local magistrates took the side of their opposition.[96]

This brings our story to early March 1765, and the start of the Conococheague uprising. Indian attacks had ceased for over half a year, but the Conococheague settlers were still fearful and angry— angry at the far-off Ohio Indians, those who might re-arm them, and the military and government they felt gave inadequate protection during recent and past attacks. The British military wanted to end Pontiac's War cheaply and quickly, and hoped that George Croghan's Indian diplomacy skills and Crown presents would bring peace. Croghan, his fellow traders, and Philadelphia merchants wanted Indian trade to open up soon. So did the Indians, and they wanted the British and their troops to leave their land. Governor John Penn was in the awkward position of trying to please everyone, and cautious of another frontier rebellion like that of the Paxton Boys.

The Conococheague uprising is well documented in newspapers, provincial government records, military and private correspondence, and James Smith's 1799 autobiography. But one needs to be wary of biases in those documents. In some cases the facts were purposely or unintentionally distorted, even in depositions given under solemn oaths "on the Holy Evangelists of Almighty God."

An almost amusing example of the latter is in Henry Prather's deposition taken on September 12, 1765, in which he discussed the sworn testimony made by two other witnesses. Prather noted that they "were only Sworn to tell the truth, and nothing but the truth, without Mentioning the whole truth," as though the absence of "the whole truth" gave wiggle room. He said one of the witnesses told him afterward that his deposition was "hard touching his Conscience," and surmised that the other had reasons to lie. However, one should also understand that Prather's interests were on the opposite side of those he was criticizing, which may have influenced his own testimony.[97]

Chapter 3

Ambush at Sideling Hill
March & April 1765

The passage of George Croghan and his packhorse train and Robert Callender's preparations at Howe's would not have gone unnoticed by the Conococheague settlers. They must have known something big was up. Someone might have seen the lead bars (used for melting into bullets) and the gunpowder barrels unless they had been carefully hidden during transport and temporary storage. However, scalping knives would play the role of proverbial cats jumping out of the bag. The March 21, 1765 *Pennsylvania Journal* published a March 14 letter from Carlisle that disclosed:

> Sometime ago Capt. Calender employed several waggons to carry Indian goods to Mr. Pollan's in Conogochieg, to be carried thence by packhorses to Fort Pitt. Unhappily the head came out of one of the barrels which was full of scalping knives (say the people) pruning knives say others, the news of this alarmed the upper end of the county, and the neighbouring parts of Maryland and Virginia, upon which advertisements were posted up, inviting all to join and prevent the carrying ammunition and such like things to the Indians, by which the frontiers had suffered so much before. (This we in Carlisle heard by the packhorse masters who came down to the settlements).[98]

On March 5, 1765, two packhorse trains left John Howe's on the Valley Road and headed onto the road towards Smith's Town. Robert Allison from Antrim, the surrounding township, led drivers and a train of 32 packhorses loaded with goods for Fort Pitt. Elias Davison, also of Cumberland County, headed a train of 49 horses. Robert Callender had contracted both of them, telling them that the goods were for George Croghan's use as Indian presents in peace negotiations. Some bundles were marked with a "BW," which all knew stood for the Philadelphia firm of Baynton, Wharton and Morgan.[99]

Allison later recalled that the invoice for his goods, which Richard Winston gave him at Howe's, listed matchcoats, shirts, strouds (woolen cloth), blankets, stockings, woman's shoes, paint, knives, and lead. The knives and lead might have been construed as weapons, but Allison did not mention gunpowder, the item of most interest to those who were searching for illegal trade goods.

The March 28, 1765 *Pennsylvania Journal* published a March 19 letter from Carlisle that gave William Smith's personal take on the events. This again clarified that the locals were concerned that ammunition as well as scalping knives were being shipped:

A few days ago William Smith, Esq; came to Carlisle, from whom we have had a very circumstantial narrative, vis. That upon the first report of goods being upon the road, the country were alarmed, hearing that a vast quantity of ammunition and scalping knives were carrying out; that many of the people had applied to him, complaining that before there was any confirmed account of a peace being established with the Indians, ammunition should be sent to them; alledging that if it had been by authority, either some of the King's troops would have escorted the ammunition or the General's orders been made known, and hence concluded that it must be the mere motion of some merchants who wanted to catch the benefit of an early commerce with the Savages. So reasoned the people. Mr. Smith advised them, not to raise any disturbance, and to satisfy themselves by enquiring of one Winston who accompanied said goods; the young man was not condescending enough to humour the people, which increased their suspicion and raised their indignation.[100]

It is not clear what route George Croghan's packhorse train took through the Conococheague settlement in February 1765. We do not know if Croghan stopped at Fort Loudoun, added some sort of military escort (beyond Lieutenant Fraser), and perhaps traveled on Forbes Road through Cowan's Gap and beyond. But we do know that Robert Callender's packhorse men went next through the region along a route to the south of Forbes Road, bypassing Fort Loudoun and not taking on a military escort, which raised suspicions as noted above. The packhorse trail they took was one ordered built by Ayr Township supervisors in 1761 as "a bridle path from Carlisle by way of Larraby's Gap [Cove Gap] to the foot of Sideling Hill, to intersect with the Provincial [Forbes] Road." The trail from Howe's connecting to this must have included the road from Smith's Town to Baltimore, which passed William Maxwell's home.[101]

When the two packhorse trains Callender hired reached William Maxwell's house on March 5, a group of several local men met them. Allison and Davison knew many of the men and identified them as: William, John, and Rees Porter, John Young, William Nesbit, James Robinson, Robert McCoy, William Dean, William McFarren, Patrick Hart and "several others." Rees Porter and Patrick Hart told them they intended to stop the goods. But instead all moved on to Smith's Town. The group of local men apparently left on foot first, because Allison said the packhorse trains passed them on the road.

At Justice Smith's house in Smith's Town, the group had grown to 50 armed men, including those that had been at Maxwell's, plus Henry Anderson, William Thyler, John McMann, Samuel Owings, "one Campbell," and Rus and William Price and Christy Hager from Maryland. William Porter, Samuel Owings, William Nesbitt and four others ran up to a packhorse driver and said if he did not stop they would blow his brains out. William Price said he had 10 Maryland men with him and they intended to "destroy the ammunition," presumably meaning gunpowder. When they found none, the crowd eventually

Justice William Smith's house, believed to have been the bottom limestone story

said they "would not molest" the trains, but warned that "the Virginians" might stop them.[102]

Elias Davison, who led one of the packhorse trains from Howe's, showed them a pass signed by George Croghan, which said the goods had Colonel Bouquet's permission to go to Fort Pitt. But the crowd questioned this pass and objected to it not having the governor's seal. They persuaded Davison to go with some of them to Fort Loudoun to have the commanding officer there attest for the validity of the pass.[103]

The above comes from three grand jury depositions given by Robert Allison and Elias Davison. William Smith gave a slightly different story in his own deposition. He testified that the packhorses arrived at the tavern of James Cunningham in Smith's Town, which was 20 or 30 rods (330 to 495 feet) from his house. Hearing the commotion, Smith left his dwelling and addressed the crowd of armed men, speaking as a justice of the peace. He said he advised them that "stopping or molesting the . . . Drivers or the . . . Goods would be a very rash & illegal act and subject the persons concerned therein to penalties & punishment." But some of the young men jeered the packhorse drivers anyway

50

and fired their guns—the first of many shots fired in the Conococheague uprising.[104]

Smith's testimony went on to relate that some in the crowd said that because peace had not been made with the Indians, it was unreasonable that their enemies should be furnished with ammunition. The provincial government expressly forbade such trade. Further, they had heard that the goods being transported to Fort Pitt were the private goods of merchants in Philadelphia who were sending them for Indian trade and thus breaking the law. The packhorse men produced a pass supposedly signed by George Croghan, but some doubted whether it was genuine. Smith was familiar with Croghan's handwriting and thought the pass's writing was different, but he "did not communicate his suspicion or doubt." Instead, he encouraged Elias Davison to go to Fort Loudoun accompanied by some of the locals to see if the commanding officer had similar orders and would sign the pass. William Morrison, David Bowen, and James Rankin went with Davison to Fort Loudoun while Allison, the drivers, and the packhorses left Cunningham's Tavern and proceeded west.

In late November 1764, after his army arrived back at Fort Pitt from the Muskingum River, Colonel Bouquet wrote to General Gage and mentioned that Fort Loudoun was garrisoned with a half company under the command of Lieutenant James Eddingstone. The half company was from the 42nd Royal Highland Regiment of Foot, whose uniform included kilts. By March 1765, Eddingstone had left for a new expedition and Charles Grant commanded the post. Grant had been demoted to ensign in 1763 when his regiment was reduced, but still retained the title of lieutenant. There seems to be no record of the exact number of troops at the fort during the Conococheague uprising. But given that a half company could be 25 to 50 men, and that the post was comfortable with sending out parties of a dozen or so men at a time, a reasonable guess is there were 30 to 40 Scottish Highlanders stationed at Fort Loudoun. In any case, it was Lieutenant Grant who met with the men who traveled the five or so miles from Smith's Town to the fort on March 5, 1765.[105]

According to William Smith, that evening William Morrison, David Bowen, and James Rankin returned and said that Lieutenant Grant told them he had received orders from Colonel Bouquet to let some goods pass. But Grant had not seen the goods that Allison and Davison were transporting and so he refused to sign the pass that Davison presented. Nevertheless, Morrison, Bowen and Rankin told Smith that Grant's response satisfied them, and that the goods should go on unmolested. Smith said he thought the men in the crowd at Cunningham's Tavern that day had returned to their homes, but heard later that some followed the packhorse train. He testified that he had no information about who was involved with the events of the next day.[106]

The rapid assembly of 50 armed men in a broad frontier community and hundreds of men in days to come required organization and leadership. James Smith credited William Duffield with raising the men who angrily confronted the packhorse trains on March 5, 1765. But soon afterwards, James Smith and William Smith would be recognized as the leaders of the Conococheague uprising.[107]

Local tradition tells us that a one-story stone house on Fritz Road today, three and a half miles southeast of Mercersburg, was William Duffield's. Local tradition also tells us that William Smith's house stood as the bottom limestone story of a two-story building on the southwest corner of Main Street and Veteran's Way in Mercersburg, until the house was dismantled in February 2011. And, Cunningham's Tavern was once at the northwest corner of Main Street and Park Avenue, where a Liberty gas station sits today. The tavern and William Smith's house were the central meeting places for settlers plotting actions during the uprising.[108]

Robert Allison led the drivers and the 81 packhorses, now combined into one train, through Larraby's (Cove) Gap, over Tuscarora Mountain, and into the Great Cove, which today is in Fulton County, Pennsylvania. The men unloaded the horses and camped for the night at or near William McConnell's tavern, a still-standing log house on Lincoln Way in present-day McConnellsburg. William McFarren and two other men met the packhorse drivers first. McFarren told Allison that there were "men coming and that they intended to stop the goods." Soon 30 to 40 more men arrived at the camp. Elias Davison also arrived that night from his meeting with Lieutenant Grant at Fort Loudoun.[109]

Allison identified some in the group to be the same men that had confronted him in Smith's Town, along with a few new faces. Among those in the crowd were William McFarren, William Duffield, Thomas Orbison, Henry Anderson, William Dean, William and Rees Porter, James McBryer, John Young, Samuel Owings, Robert Thompson, James Robinson, "two men named Semple," and "one man named Smith," presumably James Smith. Thomas Orbison told Allison that he believed the goods included gunpowder. Allison asked them not to open the goods at night, and the crowd left after "several of the party had felt and tossed about the loads."

James Smith's retelling of this part of the story paints the locals as men of reason and the packhorse men as rude jokers:

> Mr. Duffield desired the [packhorse men] to store up their goods, and not proceed until further orders. They made light of this, and went over the North Mountain [Tuscarora Mountain], where they lodged in a small valley called the Great Cove. Mr. Duffield and his party followed after, and came to their lodging, and again urged them to store up their goods. He reasoned with them on the impropriety of their proceedings, and the great danger the frontier inhabitants would be exposed to, if the Indians should now get a supply. He said as it was well known that they [the Indians] had scarcely any ammunition, and were almost naked, to supply them now, would be a kind of murder, and would be illegally trading at the expense of the blood and treasure of the frontiers. Notwithstanding his powerful reasoning, these traders made game of what he said, and would only answer him by ludicrous burlesque.[110]

The next morning, of March 6, 1765, William Duffield, Thomas Orbison and Henry Anderson returned to the camp and asked Robert Allison to inspect the goods. Instead Allison showed them an invoice and they said it satisfied them. But as they left, the men warned they were "afraid the Virginians might stop them." Allison suspected "they had some ill design" as they went off into the woods. Elias Davison recalled the three men left saying they would not stop the train, but gave a more precise warning: "the Virginians would stop him *at the foot of Sideling Hill.*" The warnings given in both Smith's Town and the camp near McConnell's Tavern show that the locals already planned to attack the train and shift the blame to others, that is "the Virginians."[111]

As reported by William Smith, "a greater part" of the crowd at McConnell's Tavern, along with Elias Davison, returned to Smith's Town that morning. In the Great Cove, Robert Allison "got the horses loaded and proceeded on with Joseph Dobson, James Wilhy and the drivers until they came to the foot of Sidelong Hill, it being near one o'clock in the afternoon." There the attack began.[112]

The exact location of this attack is not known. Contemporary accounts indicate it was near the eastern foot of Sideling Hill along the packhorse trail from McConnell's Tavern. Some have assumed that the packhorse train had reached Forbes Road, near Fort Littleton and before Sideling Hill. In any case, the attackers knew precisely where to hide and wait for Robert Allison and his packhorse train to arrive.[113]

Allison was in the rear of the train when he saw John Sampson at the front turning back with his horses unloaded. Sampson said one of his horses was shot and that "there were a number of armed and blacked men" who told him that if he did not unload his goods in 15 minutes, they would shoot the rest of the horses and the packhorse men. So they unloaded the horses as the attackers ran "around the hills, hollering and shooting." The armed men told them to take the horses and their forage and leave. Robert Callender, who was not there, later wrote to Colonel Henry Bouquet that the attackers "Called to the Drivers & said they were Virginia Volunteers who had served last Campaign under Coll° Bouquet that they had never received any Recompence for their Services, & were now Determined to pay themselves." Allison saw two horses shot, and some bundles of goods cut open and some on fire. He led his men and horses to Fort Loudoun.[114]

James Smith said he planned this attack the night of May 5, when "Mr. Duffield would not compel them [the packhorse men] to store up their goods." Smith gathered 10 men who had been in his Conococheague ranger group and they camped in the woods.

> The next day, as usual, we blacked and painted, and waylayed them near Sidelong Hill. I scattered my men about forty rod along the side of the road, and ordered every two to take a tree, and about eight or ten rod between each couple, with orders to keep a reserve fire, one not to fire until his comrade had loaded his gun by this means we kept up a constant, slow fire, upon them from front to rear. We then heard nothing of these traders' merriment or burlesque. When they saw their packhorses falling close by them, they called out 'pray gentlemen what would you have us to do?' The reply was 'collect all your loads to the front; and unload them in one place; take your private property, and immediately retire.' When they were gone, we burnt what they left, which consisted of blankets, shirts, vermillion, lead, beads, wampum, tomahawks, scalping knives, &c.[115]

Smith's men blackened and painted their faces as Indians would, but no one believed they were Indians. And few believed they were Virginians for that matter. One report identified the attackers as "English, Dutch [German] and Welsh." Their disguises were so effective that Robert Allison testified later that he could not recognize any who attacked him as being among the hostile crowds he saw the day before. The blackened faces used on this and other occasions led to Smith's men becoming known as "the Black Boys."[116]

Robert Callender was at Fort Loudoun when Robert Allison arrived with what was left of his packhorse train. After Allison briefed Callender and Lieutenant Grant, it was Callender who took charge. At Callender's request,

Grant ordered his sergeant and a squad of men to recover what goods remained undamaged at Sideling Hill. In letters Grant later sent to General Gage defending his conduct, Grant said he told Callender it was unnecessary to pay his men when Callender told them he would "give them something for their trouble" and offered a reward of £10 for every person they took who proved to be involved with burning the goods. But although Grant claimed he personally did not take any "high bribes," he admitted that: "Callender did, contrary to my Inclination, give some money openly to the Soldiers, as they had risqued their Lives, and on different Occasions Suffered a good deal of Fatigue, having also Carried the whole Goods belonging to that Company into the Fort on their Backs to prevent their being Pillaged."[117]

Sergeant Leonard McGlashan testified that he and Corporal Duncan Cameron led the 12-man squad that left for Sideling Hill to collect any undamaged goods and to "make prisoners" of anyone who "seemed likely" to have destroyed the goods. The rest of the Highlanders in the squad were John McGill, George Sutherland, Angus McKay, Donald McKay, John Corbitt, John Dure, John Cruckshanks, Lachlin McKinon, and two John McDonalds (presumably father and son). They left Fort Loudoun around 9 p.m. on March 6.[118]

A pyramid marks James Buchanan birthplace in Cove Gap, on the packhorse trail where British troops met the Black Boys.

Around midnight, the squad confronted a party of seven men in Larraby's (Cove) Gap who ran away despite Sergeant McGlashan's shouts for them to stop. McGlashan said that moonlight enabled him to see that some had new blankets wrapped around them. If not only for the late hour, the blankets made the sergeant suspicious that the men he encountered had a hand in the Sideling Hill attack. He ordered his men to pursue them up the mountain. Halfway up the mountain, McGlashan caught one man with two rifles, and his men captured another man. He left those two prisoners in the guard of Corporal Cameron and four men in the rear, while he and the other Highlanders proceeded to the top of the Tuscarora Mountain. There he saw others "creeping in the woods." As the soldiers gave chase, two of them fired their guns, contrary to McGlashan's orders. Thus the British army was responsible for the second set of shots fired in the Conococheague uprising, but no one was hit.[119]

Sergeant McGlashan and his squad continued on to McConnell's Tavern in the Great Cove, "it being the place where the rioters rendezvoused at the day they burnt the goods, as we was inform'd." Despite the early morning hour, McGlashan made inquiries and examined everyone in the place, but found none to suspect. The sergeant left his corporal and four men with the two prisoners at the tavern while the rest marched on to where the goods were damaged near Sideling Hill. They arrived there at the attack site about 6 a.m. the morning of May 7, having marched about 20 miles in nine hours overnight. After retracing their steps on their return, McGlashan and his troops had marched a total of about 40 miles and missed a night of sleep. But that was what foot soldiers did.

Robert Allison and presumably some of his horses and drivers accompanied McGlashan's troops. Allison assessed the damage and found that "out of 81 [horse] loads they were forced to leave, only about 18 loads of rum and 2 loads of dry goods and 2 loads of lead remained." That meant about 59 horse loads were lost, most burned but some apparently stolen (the blankets, scalping knife, and lead bars found elsewhere after the attack). Robert Callender, Lieutenant Grant, and others later cited slightly different amounts of lost goods (Grant wrote that 63 loads were burned), but Allison would have been the best

McConnell's Tavern still stands in McConnellsburg

witness. Grant told Colonel Bouquet that three horses had been killed and three more wounded at Sideling Hill. By good luck, or good aim, no drivers had been harmed.[120]

That day, a soldier with a letter from Lieutenant Grant arrived at Fort Bedford and briefed Lieutenant Nathan McCulloch (the post commander, also of the 42nd Regiment) of what happened at Sideling Hill. McCulloch immediately wrote to George Croghan at Fort Pitt. In this we see the death toll for horses increased, and that Grant fell for "the Virginians" ruse:

> This day a Soldier of the 42d Regmt from Fort Loudoun, informs me that the Goods for You, to be served out to Indians, were burn'd & destroy'd, (except a few Keggs) by a Sett of Villans, that attack'd the Drivers twelve Mile this side of Fort Loudoun, Those Villans disguised, by having their faces black'd, four of Your horses were kill'd, the rest were allowed with the drivers to return to Fort Loudoun . . . Mr Grant

further informs me of his being told that there were upwards of 100 Virginians to way lay them between Loudoun & this Post, this by far exceeds the Paxton affair, the consequence may be bad, in hindering Your going down the River in proper Season.[121]

Sergeant McGlashan testified that they found most of the dry goods in ashes and "a few horse loads of rum untouched" at the attack site near Sideling Hill. They (or, more likely, Allison's horses) carried the rum along with the other undamaged goods they found, back towards Fort Loudoun. At McConnell's Tavern, the rear guard and the two prisoners joined them, but Robert Allison left ahead of the soldiers. Allison met 20 armed men "near the foot of the mountain" who indicated they intended to rescue the two prisoners the Highlanders captured the night before.[122]

Following behind, on Tuscarora Mountain near where McGlashan captured his prisoner, McGlashan's party found a scalping knife they thought was "part of the goods." When they reached where they had met the men in blankets the night before, "four country men in arms" confronted the Highlanders, asking them about their business and their prisoners. When one appeared ready to rescue the prisoners, McGlashan made him a prisoner too. Next appeared a party of about 50 armed men and another argument ensued. Although outnumbered and out-armed, the Highlanders captured three more men and their guns. One last confrontation on the road led McGlashan to order his men to fix bayonets and clear a path through the protestors. Reaching Fort Loudoun, they brought in a total of six prisoners and several guns they had acquired on their mission.[123]

Grant justified his keeping the prisoners at Fort Loudoun in a March 9, 1765 letter to Colonel Bouquet: "Captain Callender thought it proper to leave the prisoners Here as the Country People is Raising in Arms and if he wou'd to take them Down [to Carlisle] I don't think it would be Safe, for the men that are Raising in Arms are determined to Rescue them if possible when they are going down to Carslisle and if they were there, it is thought, that they would Break the [jail]."[124]

Robert Callender was not through with his actions. He asked Justice James Maxwell to take a ride with him when Maxwell was at Fort Loudoun on March 7. Joined by Elias Davison and James Fleming, they rode to the house of Rees Porter, a man Callender clearly suspected as being one of the Black Boys. Callender, Davison and Fleming went into the house without a warrant or authority from Maxwell. When Maxwell eventually went in too, he saw Callender tying up Porter. Callender said he had found two bars of lead that he suspected Porter had taken at Sideling Hill. Callender took Porter to Fort Loudoun, making him at least the seventh prisoner there. When Callender called Maxwell to the fort the next day (March 8), Maxwell took the depositions of "several witnesses respecting the destruction of the . . . goods." Several of Maxwell's friends warned him that evening that a number of armed persons were about the fort with the intent of rescuing Rees Porter and the other prisoners suspected of destroying the goods, and they threatened Maxwell's life as well as Callender's.[125]

The Black Boys were not through yet, either. James Smith gathered a large group of armed men and set off to rescue the prisoners at Fort Loudoun. Lieutenant Grant wrote to Colonel Bouquet on March 9, 1765 that he heard word of 200 men coming for the prisoners and, if they were not delivered, the mob would "Burn the fort about my Ears and take them by force." He had his men "under arms" the night before.[126]

When the "multitude of armed men" arrived at the fort later that day, Grant sent out a message to have their commander speak to him. James Smith came and acknowledged he was the leader. Smith said he understood that Grant planned to send the men in his custody to the Carlisle jail and demanded their release. Grant asked what Smith's men would do if instead "the King's Troops" marched the prisoners off to Carlisle. Smith replied his party would first fire over the soldiers and then "fight the Troops & die to a Man Sooner than let them prisoners go to Goal."[127]

Threatened by the hundreds of angry armed men outside his fort, Lieutenant Grant released the men in his guardhouse on March 9. As Captain Thomas Barnsley explained to General Gage: "The prisoners that were taken have all been released on giving bail, otherwise the people was afraid it would have produced a Civil War as the people of Conococheague Settlement, a great many of which had no hand in destroying the Goods, Yet rose in a body to rescue the prisoners." Grant's explanation to Colonel Bouquet was more specific; Callender wanted them released on bail because he feared not doing so could have caused "the Country People" to "Distroy the Remainder of Goods that was Mr. Howe's." Although he let the prisoners go, Grant kept the guns collected by Sergeant McGlashan. Not sure what he should do with the five rifles and four smooth-bore guns he held, Grant made the first of several requests for direction from his superiors, asking indirectly about the guns through a March 11 letter Robert Callender wrote to Colonel Bouquet.[128]

James Maxwell identified James Smith, David Wilson, Joseph Irwin, and William Porter among those who openly avowed to rescue the prisoners and to kill Callender and himself. But after the prisoners were released on bail—on the recognizance of James Smith and David Wilson, who "undertook for their appearance at the next court to answer any charges exhibited"—Smith and Wilson told Callender and Maxwell that they had not really intended to kill them, only to beat them severely or exchange them for prisoners.[129]

James Smith wrote a different story about the events. He complained how the Highlanders took their prisoners "barely upon suspicion," and without applying to a magistrate or obtaining any civil authority first. Those in custody were "chiefly not in any way" involved with the Sideling Hill attack. Smith said he raised 300 riflemen and camped on a hill in sight of Fort Loudoun. "We were not long there, until we had more than double as many of the British troops prisoners in our camp, as they had of our people in the guard-house. Captain Grant . . . sent a flag of truce to our camp, where we settled a cartel, and gave them above two for one, which enabled us to redeem all our men . . . without further difficulty."[130]

Smith's account of capturing and exchanging troops "above two for one" does not ring true. His men would have needed to have catch 15 or more soldiers—perhaps nearly half of those garrisoned at the fort. Their capture would have been very difficult to do without bloodshed, with the soldiers so wary of the armed mob outside the fort. And it surely would not have gone unreported as it did by Lieutenant Grant, who wrote and griped about every transgression Smith and his men made.

After the release of the prisoners, the Black Boys continued to seek the gunpowder they failed to find in the packhorse train at Sideling Hill. A group from Maryland first searched Howe's (Pawling's Tavern) for ammunition but found none there on March 9. Robert Callender had indeed stored gunpowder and lead at Howe's, but moved these elsewhere among the 36 horse loads of goods he relocated, presumably before Allison and Davison picked up their goods. Callender stored six horse loads, including two barrels of gunpowder, at Robert McFarland's house. He stored the other 30 horse loads, including eight barrels of gunpowder weighing 80 pounds each and four or five horse loads of lead, at William Maxwell's home.[131]

Richard Brownson, a physician, was at William Maxwell's house on March 9, 1765 when about 20 "persons whose faces were blackened & disguised" knocked at the door and called for the master of the house. When Brownson told them the master was not at home, they said they wanted "Croghan's store of powder and lead." Then they broke open the storehouse near Maxwell's dwelling and searched the goods. Upon finding eight barrels of gunpowder, they whooped and fired a pistol in the air. This signal was answered by 20 other men at a distance, who came forward and helped move the gunpowder into the woods. Before leaving, they set fire to the barrels, which exploded. James Maxwell arrived at William Maxwell's (his father's) house after this incident and learned from Brownson what happened. Because of the men's disguises, Brownson had not recognized any of them. But he said many spoke German and, because few in Peters Township were German, he suspected them of being from Maryland or "the Borders."[132]

On March 10, Robert Callender forced a deposition from a "Mr. Volgomot in Maryland, near Potomack." Volgomot testified that a number of armed men rode by his house to and from Pennsylvania. "One Pretor" told him it was they who destroyed the gunpowder at Maxwell's.[133]

Callender's next move was to gather up the 36 horse loads of goods (minus the eight blown-up barrels of gunpowder) he had stored at Maxwell's and McFarland's and send them to Fort Loudoun for safe keeping. He also transported 19 or 20 wagon loads of his goods remaining at Howe's to the fort. One wagon load of goods from William Hueston's was sent to the fort as well.[134]

The early March 1765 events in the Conococheague settlement and near Sideling Hill had begun as a protest against private trade goods going westward to the Indians, but soon escalated into the destruction of private property, death threats, and shots fired in anger on three occasions—fortunately with only horses rather than people killed. Those in the settlement not initially riled by traders carrying "warlike stores" were sure to be upset over Robert Callender's coercion of the British troops at Fort Loudoun and their capture of fellow settlers and their guns. The settlers demanded that their peers be subject to the due process of civil law and not the whims of a trader or British troops.

The events also caused immediate concern with George Croghan at Fort Pitt, General Gage in the city of New York, and Colonel Bouquet, Governor Penn, and the merchants in Philadelphia. Their correspondence shows they were following with interest every detail of what happened and by whom.

Croghan wrote to both General Gage and Colonel Bouquet on March 12, 1765. He told Gage that he had brought better than £900 worth of the Crown presents to Fort Pitt, but much more was needed to give to the Ohio Indians he planned to meet with at the fort, as well as for his expedition "down river" to the Illinois Indians. He blamed "the insolence in the people of Cumberland County" for the loss of the rest of the Crown's presents at Sideling Hill, and for the "great uneasiness" he felt. Croghan wrote he had no doubt that Gage would "find out the perpetrators of such a Breach of the Laws and have them punished agreeable to their crimes." To Bouquet he added in his more-common poor spelling: "Such A horrad Crime Shure Neaver can be forgiven them or there Must be an End to Sivel & Military power."[135]

But General Gage had assumed that George Croghan had already taken all he needed "for Publick use" with him to Fort Pitt, and so he asked Captain Thomas Barnsley to check into the matter. Even after Gage saw the depositions of Allison and Davison, who repeated Robert Callender's story that all the goods in their 81-packhorse train were for "the Crown's use," he did not believe them. He doubted "such a large quantity of goods could belong to any others but traders."[136]

Samuel Wharton said the goods destroyed at Sideling Hill amounted to about £3000 in value, but gave differing claims as to whether or not Croghan had bought them as Crown presents. Robert Callender and John Baynton also told differing tales. At the end of March, Gage wrote to Governor Penn: "I am of opinion, when you have Examined into this Affair, that it will be found the Traders had hopes of getting first to Market, by Stealing up their Goods before the Trade was legally permitted."[137]

By June, General Gage had received bewildering bills from Philadelphia merchants for goods claimed to have been bought by George Croghan as Crown presents, including some supposedly destroyed at Sideling Hill. Gage's investigation into the bill sent by Thomas Smallman found he was not a Philadelphia merchant as the bill pretended he was; instead, Smallman was Croghan's cousin and proxy. Given lists of what were destroyed and saved at Sideling Hill, Gage said "as the King's goods were so mixed in with the traders, we have no way to ascertain whose they were that were plundered or whose property was saved." He thus delayed paying those bills until he could get a better explanation from Croghan.[138]

George Croghan and Robert Callender pressed the British army command to find and prosecute those who attacked their goods. Two days after the standoff at Fort Loudoun, in a March 11, 1765 letter to Colonel Bouquet, Callender sought praise for the two men he in fact had bossed around: "Mr. Grant & Justice Maxwell have behaved Extreamly well in this whole affair & the Governor's thanks to them in the Publick Papers might be of Real Service." But he went on to accuse William Smith: "Justice Smith has I believe rather incited those mad Peoples to do what they have Done than endeavored to Advise them from it or endeaver to Suppress them."[139]

Adamant to keep weapons and ammunition from the Indians, the Black Boys set up patrols that inspected anyone they suspected of transporting such goods. In James Smith's own words: "we kept up a guard of men on the frontiers, for several months, to prevent supplies being sent to the Indians, until it was proclaimed that Sir William Johnson had made peace with them, and then we let the traders pass unmolested." They issued passes to those whose goods met their inspections satisfactorily. Several of these passes are copied in provincial government records.[140]

Robert Smith and Francis Patterson signed one typical pass on June 1, 1765, which allowed John Gibson, four drivers, and 41 packhorses to carry supplies to Fort Pitt for use by those garrisoned at the fort. The pass acknowledged the inspection was done so "with the approbation" of local justices. Justice William Smith countersigned the pass:

> We, they Subscribers, being chosen by Jn° Gibson, with the consent and Approbation of Willm Smith, John Ranwells, and John Allison, Esquires, to Inspect a Quantity of Liquors, Dry Goods, &c., Which Goods, &c., the said Gibson is about to carry to Fort Pitt, In pursuance whereof we have Examined all the Loads Included in the Above Invoice, and have found no Warlike Stores, or any Article that in our opinion can be any Disadvantage or Enable the Indians to point their Arms against the Frontier Inhabitants.[141]

Another pass, signed by James Smith on May 15, 1765, said: "As the Sidling Hill Volunteers have already Inspected these goods, and as they are all private property, it is Expected that none of these brave fellows will molest them upon the Road, as there is no Indian Supplies amongst them." The phrase "brave fellows" became one synonym for the Black Boys and others like them on the frontier. Noteworthy also is the self-named group title "the Sidling Hill Volunteers." Although the Black Boys disguised themselves during their raids to prevent individual identification and subsequent legal action, they apparently liked having a general association with the Sideling Hill attack.[142]

The Black Boys' patrols also stopped and inspected military couriers traveling between forts and soldiers going about their business of gathering supplies. For example, William Smith signed the following pass on May 20:

Permit the Bearers, Alex[r] M'Kiney and Lachlan M'Kinnon, to pass un-molested to and from Anteiatem, they behaving themselves Soberly and inoffensively as becomes loyal Subjects, they being Soldiers Car-rying a Letter to Daniel M'Cay, and as they say, is going to purchase two Cows.[143]

The more the Black Boys interfered with trader and army operations, the more those groups complained about the "villains," "banditti," and "riot-ers" to Governor John Penn. In March 1765, as Penn was planning to come to Carlisle to invoke civil authority and find and prosecute those guilty of crimes, "Cumberland County Inhabitants" wrote him an elegant petition, apparently meant to counter what the other side was telling him. The petition told Penn of their past terror and their current fear of a third war of Indian attacks if the merchants and traders supplied them with illegal goods and ammunition:

. . . permit us honorable Sir to express to you on this occasion the alarming apprehensions which we have of being again involved in an-other war, from the unseasonable supplies of cloathing & warlike stores which we understand are preparing in great abundance, & are already on the road to the Indians, thirty thousand pounds worth of goods as we are informed by good authors, & amongst them a large quantity of ammunition; Powder, lead & scalping knives, being already in our country; & destined for the savage, faithless & unrelenting enemy, can-not but raise in our breasts the horrible images of murdered families, captivated brethren & friends, Men, Women & children, exposed to all the cruelties & Miseries which their savage dispositions can prompt them to inflict, our houses & farms involved in flames . . . But alas what does it avail us, that the French are removed out of our Country that they can no longer excite & assist the Indians, to ravage our set-tlements, & murder our friends, if our own fellow subjects regardless of his Majesties, of his Officers proclamations, nay of all the laws of god & man are still continuing to supply them with the means of our destruction? Have we with the broken remains of our dismember'd families escaped the unheard of cruelties of two Indian wars only to be involved in a third, by those very persons who have hitherto sufficiently testified the want of humanity & compassion for our distresses, do they so eagerly thirst after our blood that nothing will satisfie them but the utter distruction of our whole families, or are they so bent upon enriching themselves by an Indian trade that they will do it at the expense of so much blood & treasure as it must cost the Crown and the Colonies? . . . Permit us honorable Sir to implore your protection against the attempts of our fellow subjects who being remote from danger, sit at ease & know not what we feel, & to beseech you to interpose your Authority to stop those goods from going to the enemy until peace be finally concluded, & our friends deliver'd from their mournful captivity's & to find out & bring to punishment the persons . . . concerned in this unlawful commerce with our enemies, which has already influenced a number of people who have suffer'd greatly from the incursions of the savages to assemble in a tumultuous & lawless manner to destroy some of the goods . . .[144]

In stating their case against the traders and pleading with the governor to stop their trade, the Cumberland County petitioners also called the Black Boys' destruction of trader goods "lawless." But legal action against the latter would require they be identified and caught first.

Governor John Penn arrived in Carlisle in late March or early April 1765. Because the provincial assembly had ignored Penn's recommendation to "frame a proper Militia law," the Sideling Hill culprits had to be tried under civil law. The governor's investigation into the Sideling Hill affair and the subsequent grand jury trial is best described by Penn in a letter he wrote to General Gage on June 28, 1765:

. . . my intention of going to Carlisle, in order to get more certain Intelligence about that matter, & to take the proper Steps to bring the

Offenders to Justice. This [Sideling Hill] affair was an object of much concern to me, and I was extremely anxious to make a discovery of the Offenders, that an effectual stop might be put to any practices of the like sort for the future. I accordingly made a Journey to Carlisle, & took with me the Attorney General and two other Members of Council. On my Arrival there I immediately sent for Capt. Callender, one of the Owners of the Goods that were destroyed, to give me all the Information he could of the persons he suspected were principally concerned in the outrage, and to furnish me with all the names of ye Witnesses who could be supposed to know anything of the matter; altho' I could not gain certain proofs of the persons who committed the Fact, I caused Warrants to be instantly issued for such as were suspected, and the Sheriff was dispatched to execute them, being authorized to collect the power of the County to his aid, and instructed to desire the assistance of the King's troops at Fort Louden, if he should find it necessary. This Step, however, proved ineffectual; the suspected persons had all absconded before he arrived in the part of the County where they lived, so that not one was apprehended. In the mean time the Witnesses were sent for & examined on Oath, and I herewith send you [Gage] Copies of several of the Depositions, by which you will perceive what part Justice Smith, who is charged to have encouraged the Rioters, appear to have acted upon that occasion. All the Witnesses who were examined, as well as a number of other who were then absent, were, by my order, bound over to give Evidence at the next Court, and Bills of Indictment were accordingly present to the Grand Jury, but tho' all the Witnesses appeared and were examined by the Jury, it seems they were of Opinion that there was not sufficient Testimony to convict a single Person charged, and the Bills were returned ignoramus.[145]

Governor Penn did not stay in Carlisle for the grand jury, but he must have been disappointed to hear there were no indictments. This or later events caused Penn to declare "every man in Cumberland County was a rioter at heart and ten thousands of the King's troops could not bring one to trial."[146]

The failure of the governor to prosecute anyone for the Sideling Hill affair fueled the fire under Benjamin Franklin and others in Philadelphia who hoped to bring royal rule to the province, ousting the Penns and their governor. John Ross wrote Franklin: "if His Majesty will not Accept and take Care of this flourishing Province, it's hard to determine how such proceedings of a Lawless Mob will End."[147] Samuel Wharton gave a fuller complaint:

Our Friends wrote you fully, respecting the Insurrection in Cumberland County, When a part of the Goods, Our House was sending Out, (As I formerly informed you) To be subservient to the King's Use, were attacked and destroyed, by a Number of Irish Presbyterians. They have also doubtless, advised you, of the strange Conduct of Our Governor and Attorney Genl. Who just went to Carlisle, saw Col. Armstrong and a few Others of the prop—y Minions—sent three presbyterian Parsons and the Sheriff to Conogocheague, with a Design, as They say, To apprehend the Robbers (who returned, as Every impartial Person would privously determine, without doing any Thing) and Then, without so much, as issuing a Proclamation, or offering a Reward, for the taking Them, They returned to Philadelphia. The Consequence of all Which was, That when the Cumberland County grand Jury met, They dared to violate the Oaths, They had taken and did not find a Bill of Indictment, against any One of Them, notwithstanding the most plain and positive Proofs was adduced. In short, When We consider That almost every Man in the County, has presumed to express Himself most disrespectfully of a Kingly Government, It is not to be wondered at, If They should unite to save their Relations, from the Halter. I call Them Relations, because you may be convinced, That most of the Grand Jurors, were Relatives to some of the Robbers.

As soon as the Court broke up, all was Jollity and Uproar and They returned huzzaing to the upper parts of the County, rejoicing at their Victory Over Conscience and the Laws of their Country— When a fresh Occasion presented for Them to exercise their regulating Powers.[148]

The Black Boys continued to patrol the Conococheague roads, inspecting for "warlike goods." The Conococheague settlement escaped other noteworthy incidents until May 1765.

Chapter 4

Gunfight at Widow Barr's
May, June & July 1765

The Black Boys failed to stop and inspect a 40- to 60-packhorse train of goods before it reached and unloaded at Fort Loudoun on May 5, 1765. Perhaps the train had an armed escort or, by stealth or good fortune, its drivers avoided the Black Boys on their way to the fort. The goods belonged to Joseph Spear, who "Obtained a Permission last Winter, from the Commanding Officer at Fort Pitt, To supply that Garrison with What Necessarys, They wanted." Ralph Nailer, who led the packhorse train for Spear, described the goods as the "Great Part of them Loads was the Officers' Stores Belonging to Fort Pitt, and the Remainder was Intirely Rum, Spirrits & Wine, Except Seven Loads of Loaf Sugar, Shirts, Shoes, and other Dry Goods." When the Black Boys learned of this shipment, they became determined to inspect the goods for ammunition and weapons.[149]

In the evening after their arrival at Fort Loudoun, the drivers took the unloaded horses to pasture at Rowland Harris's place, which was a couple of miles from the fort in the mouth of Path Valley. (Harris's land was along what is now Pa. Rt. 75, a short distance north of the U.S. Rt. 30 intersection.) The next morning, on May 6, a party of about 30 armed men with blackened faces confronted the drivers and asked to whom the horses belonged and to where they were going. When told, the Black Boys said: "No One shall go to Fort

Pitt, But such as [we] admit." Other angry words ensued. The Black Boys tied up the drivers and "flogged them severely, Killed five of their horses, wounded two more, and burnt all their Saddles" and blankets. These shots fired were the fourth set in the uprising and the second set harming packhorses. One of the drivers escaped and rushed to Fort Loudoun to report the attack, and to get troops to rescue the other drivers and horses.[150]

Lieutenant Grant sent out Sergeant Leonard McGlashan with 12 other Highlanders, half of whom who had been on McGlashan's mission to Sideling Hill in March: John McGill, George Sutherland, Angus McKay, John Corbitt, the two John McDonalds, Daniel Steward, Daniel McRay, David McKenzie, Hugh Monro, and Archibald McMillon. When the troops arrived at Harris's pasture, the Black Boys were gone. McGlashan "pressed" Rowland Harris into being his "pilot" or guide. They found the Black Boys a mile or two to the south, at Widow Barr's place.[151]

The deposition of Justice John Shelby said that after the 30 or so Black Boys had left for Harris's on the morning May 6, he was in Cunningham's Tavern where another 20 armed men had gathered. The men in the tavern left and met the others (with their faces still blackened) at Widow Barr's before McGlashan showed up. Thus, by Shelby's account, there were at least 50 armed Black Boys who confronted the 13 Highlanders from Fort Loudoun.[152]

The best primary source account of the ensuing skirmish at Widow Barr's is from Sergeant McGlashan's deposition:

> upon our arrival at the Widow Barrs House they fired one Shot, supposed to be upon us; we not thinking that we were so Near them, and Looking from whence the Shott was fired we saw the party, I Call'd out to Stop, but they not Stopping one Shott was fired upon them by some of my party, in Return of which severall Shotts were fired, supposed on us, on our Retreat to the Widow Barrs; I then gave Orders to fire, and my party being on Clear Ground, and they in the Woods, obligded us to take possession of the Widow Barrs House, where we were fired upon Warmly for some time, the Black Boys being between

Seventy and Eighty in Number, as Near as I can Gues, Before we went into the House; we made one Man Prisoner, he being under Arms, and appeared as if he had been Black'd in the' face, but had attempted to Rub it off but did not do it Effectually, which Prisoner we kept about one hour, and then Released him, being perswaded by a Country Man that happened to Come there, (as he sayd by Chance) and told us that if I did not Release the afore mentioned prisoner, Neither me nor any of my party would Ever Gitt back to the Fort, upon which I Released him, and Proceeded back to Fort Loudoun.[153]

McGlashan failed to mention that he shot James Brown, one of the Black Boys, during this gun fight. Brown was wounded in his thigh, making him the only Conococheague settler casualty of the Conococheague uprising. Ironically, blood had been shed once again at Widow Barr's, where George Croghan and others had battled Indians nine years before.[154]

The house now at Widow Barr's place. The limestone part on the left was built after 1765, but the log cabin part on the right (now covered with siding) might date from the Black Boys' period.

John Shelby's deposition went on to say that after the skirmish, "the Country People all returned to Cunningham's Tavern." Shelby visited there later and heard William Smith say "it was a pitty some Man would not undertake to Settle those Highlanders for they would ruin the Country." Before May, the focus of Black Boys' anger and scorn was on traders who attempted to bring arms and ammunition to the Indians, but after the gunfight at Widow Barr's it seems to have been directed clearly towards the Fort Loudoun troops.[155]

Justice William Smith issued a warrant for the arrest of Sergeant Leonard McGlashan for wounding James Brown, and sent it to the constable of Peter's Township: "You are Hereby Commanded in his Majesty's name to apprehend him, the Said McGlasken [McGlashan], & him the said McGlasken being so taken or Delivered, you are to Bring Before me, or the Next Justice for Said County, in order to answer to Said Complaint & be farther prosecuted Against According to Law."[156]

The fact that the Black Boys knew Sergeant McGlashan's name (if not its spelling) begs the question of how well the troops and locals were acquainted with each other before their conflicts. Perhaps the Scots-Irish settlers had rubbed elbows with the Scottish Highlander soldiers in Cunningham's Tavern. Or sold them produce and livestock. Perhaps Charles Grant and James Smith had once discussed their similar experiences—both were in their twenties (Grant was born in 1740 and Smith in 1737), both had been captured by Indians, and both served on the Muskingum River under Colonel Bouquet. William Smith sent Lieutenant Grant a letter in June in which he gave Grant advice "only as a friend." Perhaps that was sarcasm, but perhaps not. But even if they had once been acquaintances or friends, the Black Boys and Highlanders now met each other with animosity, if not gunfire.[157]

Feeling defensive about his actions, Lieutenant Grant later diminished the severity of James Brown's wound and emphasized Brown's culpability in a letter he wrote to General Gage on August 24, 1765. Citing Justice Smith's warrant to arrest McGlashan, Grant said "one Brown, a Rioter . . . was perfectly Recovered some time before he [Smith] Issued the Warrant." And "Brown, who was wounded, was seen a Day or two before Blackd at the head of a party who

Search'd some Wagons, & the Morning before he was wounded he fired off his Gun as a Signal to the party to attack the pack Horses & Drivers, tho he is Represented as an Innocent Country Man about his Lawful Business."[158]

James Smith never mentioned the shootout at Widow Barr's place in his 1799 book. Perhaps he was not there; no account placed him so on May 6. Or perhaps Smith may just have been too embarrassed to write about it, given his Black Boys had the element of surprise and at least a four-to-one advantage over the squad from Fort Loudoun, and failed to shoot or capture anyone.

But James Smith was definitely present at Fort Loudoun on May 10, 1765. Lieutenant Charles Grant described how the Black Boys demanded to inspect Spear's goods stored at the fort that day:

> . . . a Body of 200 Men, as near as I could Guess, appeared before this Garrison, the above-mentioned James Smith being one of their Ring-leaders, as did likewise arrive at this Fort, the Justices Smith, Reyonald & Allison; Justice Smith & Reyonald desired that I wou'd let them inspect the Goods, & that wou'd Satisfy the Rioters. I told them that the Goods were, by the General's orders, under my Care, & that I had orders from the General at the same time to send for a Magistrate & take an Inventory of all the Goods, But cou'd not proceed upon any Such Business at a time when there was Such a Body of Armed Rioters about the Garrison, but wou'd be oblig'd to call upon Some of them next week for that purpose. To which Justice Smith made answer, that he was not Subject to the General's Orders, therefore if he did not get liberty to take an Inventory of them at that time, he would not Come again to do it. I then Shewed the Justice the orders which I had from Brigadier General Bouquet for permitting Goods to pass, as likewise the permitt Joseph Spear had from the Commanding officer at Fort Pitt for the Carrying of Goods for the Support of the Troops on the Communication; to which Justice Smith answered, that the Commanding officer's pass was no pass, and that no Military Officer's pass would do without a Magistrate's pass. Justice Smith said likewise,

that this was not a King's Fort, nor was this the King's Road, & said, that five Hundred men wou'd not Escort up these Goods without a Magistrate's pass.[159]

Justice William Smith was again asserting the power of civil law and magistrates, and threw in for good measure the facts that Fort Loudoun and Forbes Road (or specifically the part he helped build) were constructed by provincial rather than royal efforts.

In writing to General Gage about this incident, Lieutenant Colonel John Reid (army commander in the Fort Pitt district and usually called simply "Colonel Reid") wrote that he suspected the crowd gathered at the fort really intended to destroy the goods, not inspect them. "About 150 of the Rioters in Arms, Commanded as I am informed, by James Smith, and attended by three Justices of the Peace, appeared before the Fort, & demanded to Search the Goods, with an intention, it is believed, to plunder and destroy them, as they had done before." Repeating what Grant had told him about William Smith saying military passes were inadequate, Reid added: "After this declaration, it cannot be doubted that some of these Justices have encouraged the rioters & even protect them in their lawless measures."[160]

Reid's supposition that the magistrates were protecting the Black Boys is supported by the deposition of Ralph Nailer, who led Spear's packhorse train. Nailer appealed to Justice William Allen for redress over his drivers being whipped and his horses killed. Allen told him that "as there was no person Killed he [Allen] had no Business with" the case. Allen went on to express his opinion to Nailer that Spear's large train of goods was meant for more than just supplying Fort Pitt: "five or six [packhorse] Loads was Quite Sufficient for that Garrison, and not forty or Fifty."[161]

In early May 1765, at Fort Pitt, George Croghan finally convened a conference with the Ohio Indians. More than 500 chiefs and warriors of the Delaware, Shawnee and Mingo tribes attended. Croghan skillfully got them to renew their peace agreements made in 1764 with Colonel Bouquet. The Shawnees released all their white captives, as the Delawares had done earlier.

The Shawnees, who had much influence over the Illinois tribes, assigned 10 delegates to accompany Croghan on his trip to Illinois. Other prominent Ohio Indians were appointed to attend a formal peace conference with Sir William Johnson in New York.[162]

On May 12, 1765, three days before he started his journey down the Ohio River towards Illinois, Croghan wrote to Governor Penn about the success of the conference at Fort Pitt. His letter and transcripts of the meetings, and undoubtedly pressure from the British army and Philadelphia merchants, would soon convince Penn to reopen trade with the Indians.[163]

But in the meantime, the Black Boys continued their inspections. One merchant wrote in June: "The road to Pittsburg is beset by parties of our people, who declare their resolutions not to suffer any goods to go up to the Indians."[164]

On May 28, 1765, the Black Boys captured Lieutenant Grant. This time James Smith and his companions were readily identifiable, being without blackened faces. Grant told of his capture in his deposition:

> I was Riding out, & about a mile from this post as I was Coming home in Company with two other Men, was Waylay'd by five Men Arm'd, Namely, James Smith, Samuel Owens, John Piery, & two others, whose names I don't know, all under the Command of the aforesaid James Smith. Some called out to Catch me, others to Shoot me; On which I Rush'd thro' them, & on passing one of them attempted to Catch my Horse by the Bridle, Notwithstanding I passed them all; and when they saw that I was out of their hands, one of them fired a Gun, whether at me or my Horse, I cannot say, at which my horse Started into the Thickett which occasioned my falling; the Rioters then came up to me, made me as they said the King's prisoner, upon which one of them said, "take the Durk [knife] of the Rascall." I asked them for what? They said they wou'd let me know that before I wou'd go home. I asked them where they were taking me to? They said they wou'd take me before Justice Reyonald. I ask'd if it would not do as well to go before Justice Smith, being the most Convenient? They Said that their

orders was to Bring me before Justice Reyonald. They Brought me into the Woods that night Seven Miles from my post, & there Kept me all night without any Manner of Shelter; they told me that unless I would give up the Arms that I had in the Fort, that they wou'd Carry me away into the Mountains & keep me there, & that in the mean time the Country wou'd Rise & take the Fort by force of Arms, & by that means they wou'd have all the goods in the Fort as well as their Own Arms. I told them that it was not in my power to give up their Arms without orders from my Commanding officer, & told them they would be dealt with as Rebells if they would do what they threatened.

Their Commander, James Smith, said that they were as Ready for a Rebellion as we were to oppose it, & they acknowledged that their proceedings were Contrary to law; & after holding a Council Determined to go of to Carolina & take me along. They set out, & brought me about eight Miles farther. I having no Dobt but they wou'd bring me to Carolina, I ask'd them what they would have me do in the Matter, as I told them before how much it was out of my power to Deliver up their Arms? They ask'd me if I wou'd give Security to Deliver up their Arms or pay £40? To which I consented Rather than go to Carolina, on which they agreed to Bring me to an Inn at Justice Smith's, Where I gave a Bond for £40 if I did not deliver up their Arms in five Weeks.

As they were taking me away they Declared their Determination in firing upon the Troops in Case any of them Shou'd be sent in Quest of Mr. _____ . The aforesaid James Smith was the Ringleader of the party that took Serj' MaGlasken [McGlashan], belonging to the Garrison under my Command, & used him very ill.

Some days after I was Releas'd from the Rioters, I was at the House of Justice Smith, Where I met the five Men that took me & Carried me away as above Mentioned, & I told Justice Smith that those were the Men that took me away, & in what Manner they used me, But he took no Notice of it.[165]

Thus Grant identified Justice William Smith as a supporter of James Smith and the Black Boys. Grant's deposition raises a few questions. Who were the two men riding with Grant, and why did they desert him when trouble came? If James Smith and company did indeed shoot at Grant (the sixth incident of shots fired in the Conococheague uprising), then why did they not follow through and harm him after he was thrown from his horse? If the Black Boys had indeed captured Sergeant McGlashan and "used him very ill," why would they have released him when there was a warrant out for his arrest? And why would Grant visit Justice Smith's house "some days" afterwards, where he was likely to run into his abductors as he did?

In a June 7, 1765 letter, Colonel John Reid told General Gage that upon hearing Lieutenant Grant was either captured or killed, the commander at Fort Pitt sent two officers and 45 men towards Fort Loudoun. Reid met these troops on Forbes Road on his way from Fort Loudoun to Fort Bedford and told them Grant was safe, so they returned to Fort Pitt. In this letter, Reid said he had "taken to task" some of the leading men in Carlisle and near Fort Loudoun for the protection they gave the "rioters." And he also noted that William and James Smith wrote to him and "endeavored to apologize for their own conduct at the expense of the troops, but they have not proposed any satisfaction to be made for the insult offered to the commanding officer of Loudoun."[166]

James Smith and Charles Grant were not inclined to apologize to each other, as discussed in a June 17 letter addressed from Smith to Grant, but written as though meant for someone else:

> I was occasionally at Loudon a few days ago, & had the opportunity of Speaking with Mr. Grant, who told me all the Satisfaction Colonel Reid desired for taking him prisoner, was that I should acknowledge my fault to Mr. Grant, Which I refused to do, Except Mr. Grant would also Confess he had used the Country ill. This he Refused to do, & said he had done nothing but his Duty. If Colonel Reid will only say it is the Duty of an Officer at Fort Loudon, Repeatedly to send out Mr.

Grant & a party to Red [redress?] private Quarrels in the Country, I will Confess my fault to the above mentioned Gent[m]. I acknowledge my fault to Col. Reid, Beging pardon for the same. I don't accuse Mr. Grant with all the Hostilitys Committed by McGlasher [McGlashan], for I have reason to Believe McGlasher acted Contrary to his orders, & concealed many of the actions from his Commanding officer.[167]

It seems odd that after James Smith's overnight abduction of Lieutenant Grant, Grant visited William Smith's house and James Smith visited Fort Loudoun. It was as though they were taunting each other in some cat and mouse game.

Lieutenant Grant did not give up the nine firearms McGlashan confiscated in March, although he signed a bond to do so within five weeks. He felt the bond he signed while captured by James Smith was invalid because it was signed under threat. Grant seemed unsure of what to do with the guns, and kept asking for advice from his command. In August, he asked General Gage for direction: "I shoud also be glad of your Excellency's Orders with Regard to the Arms taken from the Rioters & now in the Garrison."[168]

Grant also refused to give up Sergeant McGlashan, despite the warrant for his arrest. Again he asked for Gage's advice on this, but expressed his own

Justice William Smith house undergoing deconstruction in February 2011 after efforts to save it failed.

opinion that William Smith had forfeited his right to be a magistrate through his actions, and thought a jury trial for McGlashan in Carlisle would not be fair. "[W]ho woud have got the poor Serj' Try'd by a Jury of his own adherents, with Mr. Armstrong, of Carlisle, at their head, who favours the Rioters, & woud have had no Mercy on him?"[169]

During the Conococheague uprising of 1765, William Smith's house and Cunningham's Tavern were well known as the Black Boys headquarters. On June 4, Colonel Reid wrote:

> Mr. [James] Maxwell also says that the common place of Rendezvous for them [the Black Boys] is at Justice Smith's, who he believes encourages them. I have seen some passes signed by Justice Smith and his Brother-in-law, not only for traders but even for Soldiers of the Garrison, who are not safe to go any where about their lawful affairs by a pass from their own Officers.—They use the Troops upon every occasion with such indignity & abuse that Flesh and Blood cannot bear it.—A party of them had the Impudence again to intercept the Express I mentioned in my last, in his return from Carlisle to this place, used him cruelly, and detained him all day yesterday; one Wilson, who seemed to headed the party, told the Express that they were determine to stop the Clouthing of the Regiment in its way from Carlisle.[170]

On June 4, 1765, Governor Penn and his council met to consider George Croghan's letter and transcripts on the peace meetings with the Ohio Indians. The result was Penn's proclamation reopening Indian trade after June 20, and essentially ordering the Black Boys to stop their activities:[171]

> that from and after the 20th day of June instant, all intercourse and trade with the several Nations and Tribes of Indians in amity with the Crown of Great Britain, and living under his Majesty's protection, shall be free and open to all persons residing in this Province, who shall apply for and obtaining my Licence to carry on such trade, under the

provisions and restrictions mentioned in the said Royal Proclamation [of 1763]. And Whereas . . . sundry persons have, at several times lately, assembled themselves in armed Bodies on the Western Frontiers of this Province, and have, in a most riotous and illegal manner, presumed to interrupt the passage of all kinds of Goods to Fort Pitt, by which the Garrison there hath been greatly distressed; and that small parties are now encamped and lying in wait for the same purpose, on the road of Communication to that post; I do hereby strictly charge and command all persons whatsoever, so assembled, forthwith to disperse themselves, and desist from all such illegal proceedings and practices . . . I do further enjoin & require all his Majesty's Subjects within this Government, to suffer every person hereafter travelling towards Fort Pitt with Goods, wares, or Merchandize, and having my Licence to trade with the Indians; as also, all persons transporting Goods and military Stores for the use of any of his Majesty's Garrisons, & having a passport for the same, from the Commanding Officer of one or more of the posts, to proceed and pass with the said Goods, Wares, merchandizes, & military Stores, freely and safely . . . without offering Violence or injury to their persons, or any Goods under their Charge, or giving them the least Molestation . . . I do further enjoin & require all Magistrates, Sheriffs, and other Officers, to use their utmost Endeavors at all times to quell and suppress all riots, tumults, and disorderly proceedings, tending to disturb the peace & quiet of his Majesty's Subjects, and also to be aiding & assisting in discovering & apprehending all persons that may be in any manner concerned therein, that the Offenders may be prosecuted according to due Course of Law.[172]

Sir William Johnson and the Ohio Delawares signed a formal peace treaty on May 8, 1765, which Johnson copied and enclosed in a June 7 letter to Governor Penn. Peace with the Ohio Indians and the subsequent opening of trade with them took away whatever legal or moral argument the Black Boys had for stopping, inspecting, and harassing packhorse trains carrying any kind of goods to Fort Pitt. But it would take some time before the Black Boys ceased what they had been doing since March, and for those who opposed them to accept that they had.[173]

Although based on hearsay and not as well documented as other events, there may have been another Black Boys attack on trade goods on June 7, 1765. In a letter Thomas Wharton wrote to Benjamin Franklin, he relayed what one Josiah Davenport heard on his way back from Pittsburgh. Wharton wrote:

> Our Cumberland County Inhabitants are determin'd to hinder every Supply going out to Pittsburgh; and thereby as much as possible to bring on another War, with the Indians; and for that End, to Destroy all the Goods, they can possible lay their Hands on. About the 7th of June, One Joseph Spear, was sending up, about £500 worth of Goods, to Pittsburgh, cheifly English-Manufactory; Some of those Wretches attack'd, and seiz'd the Goods; deposited them in a House, untill the 28th; Prior to which, they stuck up, several Advertizements, importing that, Those Brave-Fellows concerned in the seizing those Goods, were requested to meet and divide 'em; and that such Who inclin'd to purchase should meet with a kind Reception. Accordingly on that day it was put to the Vote, what should be done with them; and then determin'd that, they should be Burnt; which they were accordingly.[174]

Assuming that the goods of Joseph Spear delivered to Fort Loudoun on May 5 stayed safely there, a deposition by Henry Prather helps corroborate the assertion that the Black Boys captured other goods shipped by Spear. Prather's deposition told how he objected to the testimony from "one Price" (probably William Price) because of Price's "appearing Att the Head of a Riotous party at Sundry times, & for Embazelling the goods of Joseph Spears, which was Carried from or near Fort Loudoun to Maryland, & left in his Care, likewise for Carrying off a Cagg [keg] of Rum Att the Same time, when a pretence of Burning Said goods of Mr. Spears was Committing."[175]

Benjamin Franklin lost his reelection to the Pennsylvania assembly in the fall of 1764. When the Conococheague uprising broke out, he was in England pressing his futile attempt to revoke the proprietor's charter and make Pennsylvania a crown colony. As Governor Penn sought the support of Germans and Presbyterians on his side, Franklin denigrated those groups. The actions of the Paxton Boys and now the Black Boys led Franklin to exclaim the following in a June 8, 1765 letter he wrote in London:

> The Outrages committed by the Frontier People are really amazing! But Impunity for former Riots has emboldened them. Rising in Arms to destroy Property publick and private, and insulting the King's Troops and Forts, is going great Lengths indeed! . . . I can truly say it gives me great Concern. Such Practices throw a Disgrace over our whole Country, that can only be wip'd off by exemplary Punishment of the Actors, which our weak Government cannot or will not inflict.[176]

In May and June 1765, the animosity of Philadelphia merchants, shippers, the British army, and the provincial government toward the Black Boys and their supporting magistrates was very high. But beyond stopping convoys, destroying and stealing goods, killing horses, whipping drivers, kidnapping an army officer, death threats, armed confrontations, and shots fired in anger, one thing raised the acrimony even higher—an advertisement.

Thomas Romberg, the commissary of Fort Loudoun, claimed he found the advertisement posted on "the High Road" (or "Publick Road") on May 29 while out searching for the kidnapped Lieutenant Grant. He showed the original to Grant upon his return to the fort, but the original was "so much Blotted with the Durt" that he copied it and let the original be destroyed. Or so Romberg said. His "copy" of the advertisement was as follows:[177]

ADVERTISEMENT:
These are to give notice to all our Loyal Voluntiers, to those that has not yet enlisted, you are to come to our Town and come to our Tavern

and fill your Belly's with Liquor and your Mouth with swearing, and you will have your pass, but if not, your Back must whipt & your mouth be gagged; You need not be discouraged at our last disappointment, for our Justice did not get the Goods in their hands as they expected, or we should all have a large Bounty. But our Justice has wrote to the Governor, and every thing clear on our side, and we will have Grant, the Officer of Loudon, Whip'd or Hang'd, and then we will have Orders for the Goods, so we need not stop; what we have or mind and will do for the Governor will pardon our Crimes, and the Clergy will give us absolution, and the Country will stand by us; so we may do what we please, for we have Law and Government in our hands & we have a large sum of money raised for our Support, but we must take care that it will be spent in our Town, for our Justice gives us, and that have a mind to join us, free toleration for drinking, swearing, sabbath breaking, and any outrage what we have a mind to do, to let those Strangers know their place. It was first Possess, (Black's Town,) and we move it to Squire Smith's Town, and now I think I have a right to call it, and will still remain till our pleasure, and we call it Hell's town, in Cumberland County, the 25th May, 1765.

Peeters Township.

Your Scripture says 'that the Devil is the Father of Lies,' but I assure you this is the plain truth what I say.

God Bless our brave loyal Volunteers, and success to our Hellstown.[178]

The advertisement reads like a parody of a recruitment bulletin. A different advertisement was posted upon finding warlike trade goods at Howe's in March. But by May additional recruitment advertisements were not needed, not with hundreds of armed settlers showing up to protest at Fort Loudoun, or scores to harass packhorse drivers. It is clear that Thomas Romberg's advertisement was false propaganda. William Smith pursued Romberg with a court of inquiry and a warrant to make him confess to being the author of the advertisement. But Romberg swore he was not and eventually appealed to General Gage to protect him from Smith's persecution.[179]

The British army command and the Pennsylvania governor, however, took Romberg's advertisement very seriously, or at least pretended to. Lieutenant Grant sent the advertisement to Colonel Reid, who sent it to General Gage. Even before Gage had gotten his requested "full account" of the affairs at Fort Loudoun from Reid, he wrote to Reid that the crimes committed by the Black Boys "are many of them Capital, and the Gallows must be the fate of many of them."[180]

Gage attached copies of the advertisement and correspondence from Colonel Reid to Governor Penn in letter of June 16, 1765. In this letter Gage added the following, denouncing further the Black Boys and their magistrates:

> . . . the Inhabitants of Cumberland County . . . appear daily in Arms, and seem to be in an actual State of Rebellion. It appears, likewise, that the Rebels are supported by some of the Magistrates, particularly one Smith, a Justice of the Peace, and headed by his Son [rather his younger cousin, James Smith]. Unless these Insurrections are immediately quelled, and the Authors and Abettors of them brought to punishment, it is impossible to say where they will end. If the King's Troops are fired upon, and his Forts threatned with Assaults by Men in Arms, headed by Magistrates, who refuse the ordinary Course of justice demanded of them by the Officers, I can't pretend to answer for the Consequences. It belongs to you to point out the Measures proper to be taken in such Circumstances, but it is my duty to represent these matters to you, and to offer you every assistance in my power for the support of Government, and to enforce an Obedience to the Laws, both which seem in danger of entire Subversion.[181]

Governor Penn was particularly upset over the advertisement's implication that he was on the side of the rioters. Penn and his council considered Gage's correspondence, along with two letters from Colonel Reid and the advertisement, at their meeting on June 26, 1765. The result was a set of letters the governor wrote the next day to William Smith, James Maxwell, Charles Grant, and the Justices of Cumberland County. He sent copies of Reid's letters and the advertisement to all. To John Armstrong and his justices, Penn wrote a letter repeating some of the phrases used by General Gage:

I have lately received a Letter from his Excellency Genl Gage, complaining much of the riotous conduct of the Inhabitants of Cumberland; that they daily appear in Arms, and seem to be in a State of Rebellion; that they are supported in their proceedings by some of the Magistrates, & particularly by Justice Smith; that the King's troops are fired upon, and his Forts threatned with assaults by Men in Arms, headed by Magistrates . . . unless these Insurrections are immediately quell'd, and the Authors and Abettors of them brought to punishment, it is impossible to say where they will end, or what may be the consequences . . . I do require you forthwith to obtain a full and true state of those several matters, & to procure the names of the persons concerned therein, supported by Affidavits, more particularly as to the affair of making Lieut. Grant a Prisoner, and transmit the same to me. I hope my late Proclamation [of June 4, 1765] will have a good Effect in causing these Violences and Outrages to subside . . . If I find the same turbulent & unruly Spirit still continues which has actuated the people of your County for several Months past, I shall be under the disagreeable necessity of applying, in the last resort, to the General for the assistance of his Majesty's Troops, which he is ready to furnish me with to enforce my Orders, & a due Obedience to the Laws.[182]

Penn's letter to William Smith ordered Smith to appear before him in Philadelphia on July 30, 1765, to address complaints against him. Penn asked James Maxwell to appear there as a witness, and asked Lieutenant Grant to make a sworn deposition detailing "the true and exact State of this affair," charges, and the persons involved. On June 28, Penn wrote a long letter to General Gage stating the actions he had taken in the past to identify and prosecute "Rioters," and the new effort he had just initiated. Gage's response in a letter of July 5 included: "With respect to the advertisement which you resent with so much Justice, it appears to have been the contrivance of some Leader of the Rioters in order to encourage them, and to endeavour to sanctify their proceedings by every means however false audacious."[183]

Governor Penn's actions to make Indian trade legal again and to have the Cumberland magistrates investigate the charges against the Black Boys began to have their desired effect by July 1765; there seem to be no reports of Black Boy "outrages" against traders or troops in the summer and early fall of 1765. What little the official records note about the Conococheague area referred mostly to older events. It seems the farmers went back to their fields, leaving the roads to and from Fort Loudoun free for commerce and military uses.

Some circumstantial information indicates the Cumberland magistrates met at Fort Loudoun "on or about" July 18, 1765, following Governor Penn's instructions. Justices Campbell and Perry presided and examined "different Matters about Some Disturbances that had happen'd lately, likewise Concerning an Advertisement." William Smith also attended and was offended by the "Invidious Representations." Smith was further offended by Lieutenant Grant's objection to having the meeting inside the fort. Grant wrote:[184]

> . . . when the Magistrates Assembled at Loudoun, by Order of Governor Penn, to Enquire into the Conduct of some of their Brethren, they came into the Fort and Intended there to proceed to Business, But as I Observed that Several of the Rioters were present who had at different times Openly Appeared before the Fort in Arms, and who

were Called there to appear as Evidences for Justice Smith; I thought it my Duty to Object to their coming in, which gave great Umbrage to Justice Smith, who has always behaved with great Insolence to me, but was Approved of by Justice Campbell of Shippensburg, who thought I Acted with prudence, and Advised the other Justices to go to a house on the Outside of the Fort and carry on their Examination, which they did Accordingly.[185]

The exact findings of the magistrates' meeting seem to have been lost, but it is noteworthy that no prosecutions or even indictments were ever made for the Black Boys. Later, Lieutenant Grant suspected that "a Number of the Magistrates of the County have lately drawn up a Remonstrance or Something of that Kind to the Governor" with "false Assertions" against him. Perhaps these were made at the Fort Loudoun meeting and, if so, Grant would have been better off holding the meeting inside the fort where he could have listened in.[186]

The details of William Smith's meeting with the Governor on July 30 are also not known. But the meeting seems to have gone well for him because he kept his position as magistrate (for the time being) and Lieutenant Grant later fretted: "Justice Smith, who was Sent for by the Governor . . . has Returned, & . . . I'm informed, Stands in a fair light with the Governor." Perhaps Smith convinced Penn of his innocence. Or perhaps they reached a secret agreement as Penn and the Paxton Boy leaders had the year before. That is, in seeking the support of the Presbyterian frontiersmen, maybe Penn agreed to let Smith and others remain free if they would stop attacking traders and troops. If so, Smith kept his part of the bargain until November 1765.[187]

While matters were finally settling down around Conococheague Creek, George Croghan, his entourage, and presents were floating down the Ohio River in two bateaux on their way to Illinois. An attack by 80 Kickapoo and Mascouten warriors killed or wounded most in the Croghan's party and robbed them of presents, camp equipment, and money. But as Croghan recovered from his tomahawk wound, the Indians realized their mistake in killing three representatives of the powerful Shawnee nation and begged for forgiveness. In a series of meetings held near the Wabash River, Croghan skillfully got the Kickappo, Mascouten and three other Wabash tribes to agree to the British occupation of Illinois.[188]

Croghan arranged a conference with Pontiac, whom he called "an old acquaintance of mine." In July 1765, Pontiac and representatives of the four Illinois Indian nations met with Croghan and they agreed to allow the British to take over all the French forts in Illinois. Croghan, Pontiac, and the Illinois chiefs next traveled to Detroit. In a conference begun there on August 7, 1765, Croghan successfully orchestrated a peace treaty with all the Indian nations present. Although Pontiac and Sir William Johnson would not sign a formal peace agreement until the summer of 1766, Pontiac's War was essentially over, thanks to George Croghan.[189]

After visiting with Sir William at his Johnson Hall estate (near present-day Schenectady, N.Y.) in October, Croghan moved on to meet with General Thomas Gage in the city of New York. Croghan still faced charges of issuing passes allowing merchants to take illicit trade goods to Fort Pitt in March. However, Croghan was now the peace treaty hero and Gage met him with open arms. All was forgiven.[190]

In November 1765, General Gage must have been overjoyed to have the Indian war all but officially ended and could direct his attention to the growing unrest among the colonials due to the new Stamp Act. And at last the uprising of the Conococheague Black Boys was over. Or was it?

Chapter 5

Siege at Fort Loudoun
November 1765 and Beyond

The Conococheague settlement remained peaceful through the early fall of 1765. After the crops were harvested, however, the Black Boys' thoughts turned back to the five rifles and four smoothbore guns held at Fort Loudoun since March. Word had spread to them that Lieutenant Charles Grant and his troops were about to abandon the fort and be stationed farther west. They feared Grant would take the guns with him. Grant had finally gotten direction from his superiors to hold on to the arms until the governor asked for them. Grant was not inclined to give them directly back to the Black Boys, the men he now despised.

This all led to the third confrontation between Black Boys and British troops at Fort Loudoun. Lieutenant Grant described what happened in a November 22, 1765 letter to Colonel Reid:

On the 16th Instant, a man came in from the Country, and told me that there was Three Different Party's waiting about the Fort, to take Me and Mr. [Mc]Glashan Prisoners, as they heard we were to March soon; at 7 o'clock at Night, the Fort was Surrounded by a number of the Rioters, who kept firing and hooting the whole night; next day they got more men and encampt round the Fort, so that nobody could come in or go out of the Fort; they Began next night and kept firing till Day light, when they sent me word that they wanted their Arms to be delivered to the Magistrates. I told them that I did apply to the Justices, but that they refused to take the Arms; at 10 o'clock they appeared to the number of about 100, and fir'd upon all Corners of the Fort, so that the Centry's could not stand upright upon the Bastions; they kept firing at the Fort to one o'clock, when Mr. M'Dowell came in, and said, if I would let him have the Arms, that he would give me a Receipt, and that those Arms would remain in his House till such time as the Governor would give Orders about them, and that the owners would be satisfied whatever the Governor thought proper to do with them.

As the General wrote to me to give up the Arms when the Governor would desire it, I condescended so much as to take Mr. McDowell's Receipt, that the Arms would not be delivered up to the Owners, till the Governor would desire it, as the Garrison was much fatigued for want of Sleep for two nights and two days before, owing to the Rioters firing on the Fort. I thought it best to give the Arms to Mr. M'Dowell, as I had no particular orders for carrying them with me. I was not sure when I would have a Reinforcement, but two hours after I settled with Mr. M'Dowell, Mr. Herring come with 30 men, but I thought it would not be worth the while to take the Arms again, as they were as safe with Mr. M'Dowell, as if I had taken them to Fort Pitt. I inclosed to you a copy of an Obligation Mr. M'Dowell has from some of their Head men, shews that they have Authority to sett those men to do any thing. James Smith headed those Rioters that fired at the Fort, and headed the three Party's that were waiting to take me, and to take Mr. Glashan Prisoner.[191]

Captain William Grant, of the 42nd Regiment and commander at Fort Pitt, wrote to Colonel Reid on November 25 and noted that it was he who sent Ensign Peter Herring and 30 men to escort the Fort Loudoun troops to Fort Pitt. Captain Grant's version of what Lieutenant Grant said increased the

Two views of Fort Loudoun, reconstructed in 1993

number of Black Boys to 200 or more, and gave additional details of the siege and shooting (the seventh, greatest, and last shooting incident of the Conococheague uprising):

> . . . [Lieutenant Grant] was Besieged for two Nights and two Days; the Rioters fired some hundreds of Shot at the Stockades, and in return, one of his Sentries fired only one Single Shot, this Sentry was personally fired at three different times, which at last provoked him to fire a shot; many Balls went through Patton's House, and many Lodged in the Stockades of the Fort. Lieut. Grant had but little Ammunition, which made him Cautious to fire till the Lawless Scoundrels would come close to the Fort, the Villians Encamped at Night round the Fort, lighted Fires; Mr. Grant counted Twenty, and he believes the number of the rioters might Exceed Two Hundred. In this affair, Justice Smith proves himself to be a most Atrocious Scoundrel . . . [192]

The receipt Justice William McDowell signed for the guns said: "Received of Lieutenant Charles Grant, of the 42 Regiment, the number of Five Rifles and Four Smooth Guns, which was taken off the Country People, & I promise that the above mentioned Arms shall remain in my possession till the Governor's Pleasure is known to Dispose of them as he shall see fit, either to the Respective Owners or otherways." The copy of this receipt in the Pennsylvania archives is dated "10th November, 1765," which must have been a mistake. Two related bonds were signed on November 18, confirming Grant's date as when McDowell received the guns.[193]

In one of these bonds, Jonathan Smith, William Marshall, Thomas Orbison, and John Welsh, all of Peters Township, bound themselves for £200 on the condition they "keep the said Wm. M'Dowell indemnified from any Assault, Arrest, Attachment, or Suit at Law . . . on the account of Five Rifles and Four Smooth Bored Guns . . . untill the Governor's pleasure be known concerning the said Guns." The governor later clarified that "his pleasure" was to return the guns to their owners. In the other bond, James Smith and Samuel Owens agreed to pay Charles Grant £500 if they did not "disperse immediately from this Post, without any injury or assault to any Person or Persons, and we do hereby further promise, that we shall not interrupt or insult any Person or Persons hereafter, in going up or coming down."[194]

General Gage recognized that the November siege at Fort Loudoun could have turned out much different. In a December 13, 1765 letter to Governor Penn, Gage again expressed his outrage at "one of the same Scoundrels, called Smith, and his rebel clan" and noted:

If any shadow of Law or Justice remains in Pennsylvania, I am confident that you will leave no method untried to bring these lawless Villains to condign punishment. I have not heard that any man has been killed, & it may, therefore, be better that the Officer prevented his men from Firing, but if he had returned the Fire of those Ruffians and killed as many as he was able, I conceive he would have acted consistent with the laws of his own & of every other civilized Country.[195]

Governor Penn and his council considered Gage's letter when they met on January 10, 1766. The council advised the governor to take action against William Smith and James Smith:

> . . . that William Smith, Esqr, one of the Justices of the Peace for the County of Cumberland, has, in the course of the Transactions of the Rioters there, been very negligent in his duty in not using his best endeavours to put a stop to their illegal Proceedings; but on the contrary, in favouring and countenancing them in a manner tending to reflect great dishonour on the Government. The Council, therefore, advised the Governor to issue a Supersedeas to remove the said William Smith from the Magistracy, and also, to desire the Chief Justice to send a Writ, directed to the Sheriff of Cumberland, for apprehending James Smith, one of the Principals & Ringleaders of the Rioters in the said County.[196]

On January 15, 1766, Governor Penn issued a supersedeas, suspending William Smith as a magistrate. Penn wrote back to General Gage on February 10 noting this action, and that:

> The Chief Justice has also issued a Writ for apprehending James Smith, their head & Ringleader, which has been transmitted to the Sheriff of Cumberland, to be duly executed. I have not yet heard of his success, but would fain hope that Villain may be taken, and we shall be able, by his means, to discover and take some of the other principals.[197]

General Gage wrote to Governor Penn on February 17, 1766:

> I . . . am greatly obliged to you for the pains you have taken to bring the Offenders concerned in the Riots at Fort Loudon to Justice, which will be the best means to prevent such Lawless proceedings for the future. And I shall take care that the Highland Regiment is informed

of your Intentions in this respect, as I must confess to you I think it necessary to take some Precautions to prevent Misschief in case that Regiment should pass the Frontiers of Pennsylvania.[198]

The transfer of captured guns to William McDowell and the evacuation of troops from Fort Loudoun marked the end of the Conococheague uprising of 1765. However, as noted in General Gage's letter, the Black Boys continued to be thought of as a threat. On March 2, 1766, Robert Callender wrote from Pennsborough to the firm of Baynton, Wharton, and Morgan and expressed his concern that trading goods meant for George Croghan to take to Illinois would be attacked on their way through the Conococheague settlement:

> Since my return home, I have been informed by sundry persons, that the rascally part of the Inhabitants of Conegocheage are determined, and now laying a plan, to do you some piece of injury, by either stopping or destroying some part of your last Cargo that yet remains with the Carriers in that Neighborhood, on account of Justice Smith's discharge from the Magistracy, for which they entirely blame your House, thinking that it is you alone have excited the Governor to do it. As you have already experienced so much of their Villainy, they are not to be trusted farther than seen, and therefore I have advised Irwin to go immediately up to that Neighborhood, and stop the proceedings of the Carriers till there is some methods fixed upon for the safe Conveyance of these Goods, now in their Charge, least the Devil should tempt them to commit some Outrage of that kind, which I have great reason to believe they will.[199]

Samuel Wharton gave this letter to Governor Penn as he arrived to meet with his council on March 6, 1766. On the advice of his council, Penn wrote letters that day to John Armstrong and the other magistrates in Cumberland County and to General Gage. To the magistrates, he passed on Callender's suspicions of further attacks by the Black Boys and ordered:

if you shall hear that any of the people are assembling for such unlawful purposes, you are immediately to call to your Assistance the Sheriff and power of the County to prevent the Execution of their designs; but in case the fullest Exertion of your Authority and Influence should not be sufficient, I require you forthwith to give me information thereof, that I may Order some of the King's Troops to the Aid of the Civil power, in compelling the people to submit to the Legal Authority of the Government, & pay due Obedience to the Laws.[200]

To General Gage, Penn relayed what he had written to the Cumberland County magistrates and added:

lest the force of the civil Government should not be suffice to answer the purpose, I must beg the favour of your Aid, and that you will be pleased to furnish me as soon as Possible, with your Instructions to the Commanding Officers of the King's Troops at Lancaster, & the different Posts on the Communication to Fort Pitt, to obey such orders as I may, from time to time, be under the necessity of giving them for preserving the Public peace, and supporting the Laws, as well as the Dignity of his Majesty's Government, committed to my Care.[201]

Penn's orders and the proposed counter measures by the sheriff and the British army proved to be sufficient in preventing any further Black Boy disruptions. Or perhaps the Conococheague settlers had just finally calmed down now there were no more Indian attacks, Indian trade was legal again, and those hated troops at Fort Loudoun had left for good. In any case, there were no further reports of Black Boy disturbances in the Conococheague settlement.

Pennsylvania experienced at least one more incident of mass Scots-Irish lawlessness on the Cumberland County frontier. Frederick Stump lived on Middle Creek (near present-day Selinsgrove) in what was then the northern part of the county. In January 1768, he was visited by six Indians whom he killed after getting them drunk. The next day Stump traveled up the creek with his 19-year-old servant, John Ironcutter, where they killed one Indian women and three children. Stump freely admitted his crimes and Governor Penn offered reward of £200 for his arrest and conviction.[202]

Stump and Ironcutter fled but were caught and placed in the Carlisle jail. Chief Justice William Allen issued a writ for their transportation to Philadelphia for trial, but Justice John Armstrong refused to comply with the order, insisting on having a local trial. Penn sent Armstrong a nasty and threatening letter but too late to make a difference. That is, on January 29, 1768, a group of about 80 armed men broke into the Carlisle jail and freed Stump and Ironcutter. They were never caught again.

The assembly blamed the continued defiance of laws in Cumberland County on Penn's failure to prosecute the Paxton Boys. Penn publicly denied that, but two years later he privately said some of "those who murdered the Indians in Lancaster" had "rescued Stump out of Carlisle Gaol."

Historian Robert Crist wrote that the Pennsylvania frontier was not greatly disturbed by the events that led up to the American Revolution. "The west stayed calm during the east's storm over the Stamp Act, the tea monopoly, and the taxes of the Townshend duties, rising up only when its civil rights were threatened, as in the case of the Black Boys, Paxton Boys, and Stump-Ironcutter incidents." But when the call for arms came two weeks after the battle at Lexington and Concord, "representatives of nineteen Cumberland County townships met [on May 4, 1775] in response to a call from the First Congress to form companies of 'Associators.' Cumberland reported that about 3,000 men enlisted, a figure to be compared with the quota for the entire province, which was only 4,300."[203]

William Smith never became a magistrate again. If he did indeed have a secret agreement with Governor Penn, the November 1765 siege at Fort Loudoun apparently broke it. William Smith died at age 47, on March 27, 1775. His son William inherited his tract of land and laid out the town of Mercersburg on March 17, 1786.[204]

The sheriff did not arrest James Smith. At the end of June 1766, Smith had left the Conococheague settlement to explore Tennessee. James Smith led

Portrait believed to be Colonel James Smith in old age
(Courtesy of the Eva G. Farris Special Collections,
W. Frank Steely Library, Northern Kentucky University)

a long and very colorful life. The events of the Conococheague uprising of 1765 take up only five of the 161 pages in his 1799 autobiography (and one page of the five is for a song—see Appendix 1). Smith wrote nothing about the November 1765 siege and the release of the guns. Instead he gave a somewhat remorseful statement: "The king's troops, and our party, had now got entirely the out of the channel of civil law, and many unjustifiable things were done by both parties. This convinced me more than ever I had been before, of the absolute necessity of the civil law, in order to govern mankind." James Smith served as a colonel in the Revolutionary War. He died in Kentucky in 1812.

John Armstrong became a brigadier general in the continental army and a major general in the Pennsylvania militia during the American Revolution. He led troops at the battles of Brandywine and Germantown. Armstrong served in the Continental Congress from 1777 to 1780 and later in the Congress of the Confederation in 1787 and 1788. He died in Carlisle in 1795.

George Croghan returned to Illinois in 1766, bringing trade goods from Baynton, Wharton and Morgan. He kept his position as deputy Indian agent while pursuing illicit Indian trade and land speculation schemes. Croghan died in 1782, leaving behind little money but many land deeds, which became subject to numerous lawsuits.

Benjamin Franklin's scheme to oust the Penns and make a royal province out of Pennsylvania failed. Governor John Penn remained in his office until 1771, when he left to take over his deceased father's role as part-proprietor. Penn returned as lieutenant governor in 1773 and served until 1776 when the American Revolution forced him out. He lost the unsold lands of his proprietorship. However, he signed a parole and a loyalty oath that allowed him to keep his private property. John Penn died in Pennsylvania in 1795.

Colonel Henry Bouquet stayed in Philadelphia until promoted to brigadier general in command of the southern district forces in May 1765. When he moved to Pensacola in Florida, he contracted yellow fever, dying of the disease in September 1765, without ever returning to his Conococheague home.

Lieutenant Charles Grant remained in the British army and fought during most of the Revolutionary War. He was promoted to captain in 1784, and died at age 44 in 1785.

General Thomas Gage, his American wife, and their children sailed to England in 1773. They came back to colonies the next year when he was appointed governor of Massachussetts. It was General Gage who sent 700 British troops to Concord to take militia supplies, resulting in the battle of Lexington and Concord and the start of the Revolutionary War. Upon request, Gage returned to England in September 1777, where he died in 1787.

The 42nd Royal Highland Regiment, "The Black Watch," left America to be stationed in Ireland. It returned during the Revolutionary War and fought in the battles of Long Island, Brandywine, and Monmouth. It remains an active British military unit today.

Chapter 6

Not a Rebellion
Summary and Conclusions

The very long title of Neil H. Swanson's partly fictional 1937 book about James Smith begins *The First Rebel - Being a Lost Chapter of our History and a True Narrative of America's First Uprising against English Military Authority and an Account of the First Fighting between Armed Colonists and British Regulars Together with a Biography of Colonel James Smith* (the title continues beyond this). Swanson and others since have emphasized the three "Firsts" in his title. They make the case that the first blood shed in combat between colonists and the British army was at Widow Barr's in 1765, rather than at Lexington and Concord in 1775. Some have gone as far as claiming that the "Black Boys Rebellion" was the beginning of the American Revolution. But was the Conococheague uprising a true rebellion and, if so, what was it rebelling against?

The Black Boys were well organized—a desirable attribute of any uprising or rebellion. Scores to hundreds of armed men showed up simultaneously to attack packhorse trains or surround Fort Loudoun. They systematically regulated both private and military convoys, performing inspections and issuing passes. Many of the local magistrates supported the Black Boys and allowed a good bit of their lawlessness before Governor Penn opened up the Indian trade again and directly ordered them to quell the "rioters."

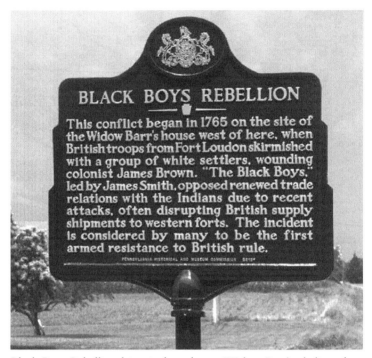

BLACK BOYS REBELLION

This conflict began in 1765 on the site of the Widow Barr's house west of here, when British troops from Fort Loudon skirmished with a group of white settlers, wounding colonist James Brown. "The Black Boys," led by James Smith, opposed renewed trade relations with the Indians due to recent attacks, often disrupting British supply shipments to western forts. The incident is considered by many to be the first armed resistance to British rule.

PENNSYLVANIA HISTORICAL AND MUSEUM COMMISSION 2013

Black Boys Rebellion historical marker at Widow Barr's, dedicated on June 23, 2013. The historical marker is a registered trademark ® of the Pennsylvania Historical and Museum Commission and the marker is copyright protected. Used with permission.

Contemporary accounts show the word "rebellion" was indeed used. Lieutenant Grant said James Smith told him the Black Boys "were Ready for Rebellion." And when Governor John Penn wrote to John Armstrong and his justices, he passed on General Thomas Gage's complaint about "the riotous conduct of the Inhabitants of Cumberland . . . they daily appear in Arms, and seem to be in a State of Rebellion." But "ready for" and "seem to be in" rebellion are not the same as saying a rebellion was actually underway.[205]

Thomas Romberg's dubious "advertisement," which both Gage and Penn treated as genuine, had a rebellious tone. But, in contrast, the March 1765 petition actually written by Cumberland County inhabitants was a respectful plea for the governor to enforce his own ban on trading warlike items to enemy Indians. It was neither threatening nor advocating the overthrow of the provincial government. Instead, Benjamin Franklin and others in Philadelphia were plotting such an overthrow.

Eleanor Webster's evaluation of the Conococheague uprising called it an "insurrection" and a "rebellion," but concluded it "was not politically oriented nor were its leaders interested in achieving political goals." And "James Smith and his 'Black Boys' were not rebelling against either the provincial or the royal governments." The Black Boys sang they were acting "for their King and their country's good" (see Appendix 1). If one accepts another Webster's (the dictionary's) definition of a rebellion as "an uprising or organized opposition intended to change or overthrow an existing government or ruling authority," then the Conococheague uprising of 1765 was not a rebellion.[206]

The initial focus of the Black Boy's actions was to stop illicit trade items from going west. They caught George Croghan and Robert Callender in their lie about Indian trade items being transported for Crown use. Had Lieutenant Charles Grant not been deceived, bullied or bribed into assisting in their lie and had instead followed his orders more strictly, the British army may never have gotten involved.

But instead Grant followed Callender's directions and ordered his troops to retrieve the undamaged goods at Sideling Hill and capture suspects. The Conococheague settlers and their magistrates saw the local troops imposing military force where civil law should have ruled. This created grudges that grew into a feud between the Black Boys and Lieutenant Grant and Sergeant McGlashan. The British army command, up through General Gage, became outraged by the Black Boys' actions. However, the Black Boys' acrimony seemed focused on what the Fort Loudoun troops had done and not the British army as a whole. Had Lieutenant Grant wisely given up the captured guns as he did his prisoners, he would not have been kidnapped and there would have been no final siege at Fort Loudoun.

The Conococheague uprising of 1765 lasted eight months, from the Sideling Hill attack in March to the Fort Loudoun siege in November. It resulted in the destruction and theft of property and disruption of military operations. The uprising caused much concern within the Conococheague settlement and at the highest levels of the British army and provincial government. However, because of either extraordinary restraint and control by the participants, or just a series of lucky near misses, only horses were killed. Human injuries amounted to the whipping of some packhorse drivers and a bullet wound in one Black Boy's thigh.

We can ponder what might have happened if there had been more significant consequences. What if any of the seven shooting incidents, comprising hundreds of rounds fired in anger, had resulted in more than just the wounding of James Brown? What if Ensign Herring and his 30 troops arrived at Fort Loudoun a few hours earlier, before Grant had turned over the guns and the Black Boys were still shooting at the fort?

It is easy to imagine that much greater casualties of civilians and British troops could have occurred and eclipsed later events like the Boston Massacre in 1770 and perhaps approached the bloodshed at Lexington and Concord in 1775. And if so, the faux-Indians at Sideling Hill in March 1765 might be as well remembered today as those in the Boston Harbor in December 1773. But the casualties of the Conococheague uprising were relatively minor (although horse lovers might not think so) and so today the Conococheague uprising generally gets its place in history sandwiched between the other two Scots-Irish uprisings in Pennsylvania—the Paxton Boys and the Stump/Ironcutter massacres.

The Black Boys had some similarities to the Paxton Boys and those who broke Stump and Ironcutter out of jail. The frontiersmen in Cumberland and Lancaster Counties were largely Scots-Irish Presbyterians who felt alienated from the Quaker-dominated assembly in Philadelphia, which they believed had spent too little on their defense against Indian attacks. This blame was a little unjustified in that many Quaker assemblymen voted to raise militias, support the provincial army, and build forts during Pontiac's War, whereas it was the parsimony of the Penns that sometimes blocked defensive actions that would have taxed their own lands. The frontiersmen also did not fully appreciate the broader approach of the British and provincial armies, which took troops out of their regions to bolster Fort Pitt and its line of communication, and to campaign in Ohio. Hundreds deserted the provincial forces during Bouquet's Ohio campaign.

The "Boys" stressed that civil law be enforced, insisting that their people be tried in local courts by their peers and not be incarcerated in Philadelphia or on an army post. The Black Boys in particular objected to military rule and even insisted that supplies for the army have approval from local magistrates to pass through their region. But although they could justify their actions to themselves, the so-called "banditti" and "rioters" realized that many of their deeds were unlawful. James Smith admitted that his group "got entirely out of the channel of civil law." Both he and William Smith apologized for some of their group's actions.

Of course all the frontiersmen feared and hated the Ohio Indians who repeatedly had killed and captured family members and neighbors. However, those tribes lived far off and out of reach. The big difference between the actions of the Black Boys and the Paxton Boys and Frederick Stump is that the latter took out their frustrations and anger on neutral and peaceful Indians whereas the Black Boys took out theirs on traders and troops.

James Smith's adoption into an Indian family gave him a good understanding and appreciation for that race. His 1799 *Account* and his 1812 *Treatise* show great respect for Indians. Both James Smith and William Smith seem to have been much more reasonable and compassionate men than Frederick Stump or Lazarus Stewart, who led the Paxton Boys both in Lancaster and later in the Wyoming Valley. But we should also recall that James Smith campaigned as a soldier against Indian enemies, and led a scalping party that presumably would have killed and taken the scalps of non-warriors as well as warriors if it had found any. The most obvious reason why the Black Boys refrained from killing any Indians living in the Conococheague settlement is that apparently none were there.[207]

The legacy of the Black Boys is that they banded together and took great risks to protect the Conococheague settlement from future harm. They prevented arms and ammunition from reaching the Ohio Indians before peace was finally settled. We will never know what would have happened if the traders dispersed their "warlike goods" earlier. But we do know that the Indian violence that was so prevalent in 1764 and before ceased forever in the Conococheague area. With peace restored to the Conococheague, prisoners and guns released, and no legal repercussions except the loss of William Smith's magistrate position, the Conococheague uprising of 1765 can be considered a rousing success.

Ye Patriot Souls Who Love to Sing

James Smith's 1799 book contains the following lyrics about the Black Boys' exploits. Smith said the song was composed in 1765 "by Mr. George Campbell (an Irish gentleman, who had been educated in Dublin) and was frequently sung to the tune of the Black Joke." The "Black Joke" or "Black Joak" was a bawdy tavern song of the early eighteenth century.

Music notation and first stanza lyrics (*next page*) provided by the Greenwood Muse Ensemble. *Above*, Jeff Greenawalt of the Ensemble. Photo courtesy Greenwood Muse, www.facebook.com/pages/Greenwood-Muse-Ensemble/148656971824051

Ye Patriot Souls

To the tune of Black Joke

words George Campbell

arr. by Sharon Nelson
of Greenwood Muse

Ye patriot souls who love to sing,

What serves your country and your king,

    In wealth, peace, and royal estates,

Attention give whilst I rehearse,

A modern fact, in jingling verse,

How party interest strove what it cou'd,

To profit itself by public blood,

    But, justly met its merited fate.

Let all those Indian traders claim,
Their just reward, inglorious fame,
      For vile base and treacherous ends.
To Pollins, in the spring they sent,
Much warlike stores, with an intent
To carry them to our barbarous foes,
Expecting that no-body dare oppose,
      A present to their Indian friends.

Astonish'd at the wild design,
Frontier inhabitants combined,
      With brave souls, to stop their career,
Although some men apostatized,
Who first the grand attempt advis'd,
The bold frontiers they bravely stood,
To act for their King and their country's good,
      In joint league, and strangers to fear.

On March the fifth, in sixty-five,
Their Indian presents did arrive,
      In long pomp and cavalcade,
Near Sidelong Hill, where in disguise,
Some patriots did their train surprise,
And quick as lightning tumbled their loads,
And kindled them bonfires in the woods,
      And mostly burnt their whole brigade.

At Loudon, when they heard the news,
They scarcely knew which way to choose,
      For blind rage and discontent ;
At length some soldiers they sent out,
With guides for to conduct the route,

And seized some men that were traveling there,
And hurried them into Loudon where
     They laid them fast with one consent.

But men of resolution thought,
Too much to see their neighbors caught,
     For no crime but false surmise;
Forthwith they join'd a warlike band,
And march' d to Loudon out of hand,
And kept the jailors prisoners there,
Until our friends enlarged were,
     Without fraud or any disguise.

Let mankind censure or commend,
This rash performance in the end,
     Then both sides will find their account.
'Tis true no law can justify,
To burn our neighbors property,
But when this property is designed,
To serve the enemies of mankind,
     It's high treason in the amount.

Appendix 2

Black Boys and Magistrates

Records from 1765 frequently mentioned James Smith and Justice William Smith as the leaders of the Black Boys. Justice William Maxwell was also frequently mentioned as an opponent of theirs.

Out of the hundreds of other men who served with the Black Boys, and the several who were involved as magistrates, those listed below are specifically named in the contemporary records.

Black Boys	Notes on when & where identified
Anderson, Henry	b, d, e
Bowen, David	b, c
Brown, James	h
Campbell, "one"	b
Dean, William	a, b, d
Duffield, William	d, e, m
Hager, Christy	b
Hart, Patrick	a,b
Irwin, Joseph	g
Marshall, William	l

McBryer, James	d
McCoy, Robert	a, b
McFarren, William	a, b, d
McMann, John	b
Morrison, William	b, c
Nesbit, William	a, b
Orbison, Thomas	d, e, l, m
Owings (Owens), Samuel	b, d, i, l
Patterson, Francis	j
Piery, John	i
Porter, John	a, b
Porter, Rees	a, b, d, f
Porter, William	a, b, d, g
Price, Rus	b
Price, William	b, k
Rankin, James	b, c
Robinson, James	a, b, d
Semple, "two men named"	d
Smith, "one man named"	d
Smith, Jonathan	l
Smith, Robert	j
Thompson, Robert	d
Thyler, William	b
Welsh, John	l
Wilson, David	g, n
Young, John	a, b, d

Notes

a = at William Maxwell's on March 5, 1765

b = at Smith's Town on March 5, 1765

c = went with Elias Davison from Smith's Town to Fort Loudoun on March 5, 1765

d = at McConnell's on March 5, 1765

e = at McConnell's on March 6, 1765

f = imprisoned by Robert Callender on March 7, 1765

g = at Fort Loudoun to rescue prisoners on March 9, 1765

h = shot at Widow Barr's on May 6, 1765

i = with James Smith in kidnapping of Lt. Grant on May 28, 1765

j = signed pass to allow goods of John Gibson to pass on June 1, 1765

k = accused of stealing goods from June 7, 1765 attack on Spear's train

l = signed bond at Fort Loudoun in November 1765

m = seen with armed men by John Shelby at Cunningham's tavern, "some time after" Widow Barr's shootout

n = Colonel Reid wrote on June 4, 1765 of "one Wilson" in charge of a group that detained his messenger

Magistrate (Justice)	Notes on when & where identified
Allen, William	bb
Allison, John	aa, cc
Campbell	dd
McDowell, William	ee
Perry	dd
Ranwells, John	cc
Reyonald	aa
Shelby, John	ff

Notes

aa = at Fort Loudoun on May 10, 1765

bb = refused Ralph Nailer's request for redress from attack at Harris's in May 1765

cc = gave approbation to inspect John Gibson's goods on June 1, 1765

dd = presided at magistrates' meeting at Fort Loudoun on or about July 18, 1765

ee = received and signed receipt for guns at Fort Loudoun in November 1765

ff = witnessed Black Boys at Cunningham's Tavern on May 6, 1765 and afterwards

Notes

CHAPTER 1   Indians, Settlers and the French & Indian War

1. James D. Rice, *Nature & History in the Potomac Country*, Baltimore, 2009.
2. Woman's Club of Mercersburg, *Old Mercersburg*, New York, 1912, pp. 19- 21.
3. Although some writers have assumed that he was a native of the Conococheague settlement, more likely James Smith (1737-1812) was from Chester County, Pennsylvania, like his cousin William Smith (c.1728-1775), per G. O. Seilhamer, *The Bard Family*, Chambersburg, Pa., 1908, pp. 456-457, *Old Mercersburg*, p. 20.
4. Kerby A. Miller, Arnold Schrier, Bruce D. Doling, David N. Doyle, editors, *Irish Immigrants in the Land of Canaan*, New York, 2003, Chapter 21, "James McCullough 1748-1758," pp. 156-179.
5. Warner, Beers & Company, *History of Franklin County*, Pennsylvania, Chicago, 1887, p. 160.
6. John Graham Palmer, *The Palmer Papers*, unpublished with copies at the Conococheague Institute library, pp. 1483-1484, 3044.
7. C.A. Weslager, *The Delaware Indians; A History*, New Brunswick, NJ, 1972, pp. 214, 218.
8. The chief representatives of the proprietors in the colonies where usually lieutenant or deputy governors, but were commonly called "Governor." That convention will be followed in this book.
9. *Minutes of the Provincial Council of Pennsylvania (MPCP)*, Vol. VI, Harrisburg, 1851, pp. 130-131.
10. Weslager, *The Delaware Indians*, pp. 209, 224-226.
11. Walter Isaacson, *Benjamin Franklin, An American Life*, New York, 2003, pp. 166-169.

12. Isaacson, *Benjamin Franklin*, p. 167.
13. Seilhamer, *The Bard Family*, pp. 454, 457.
14. *MPCP,* Vol. VI, p. 466-467. James Smith, *An Account of the Remarkable Occurrences in the Life and Travels of Col. James Smith*, reprinted Cincinnati, 1870 (originally printed in Lexington, Kentucky, 1799), pp. 5-6.
15. Smith, *An Account.* Smith wrote his book in 1799, many years after the events he discussed occurred. Historians have questioned the validity of a few events for which potential corroborating witnesses failed to confirm what Smith wrote. Ian K. Steele (in *Setting All the Captives Free: Capture, Adjustment, and Recollection in Allegheny Country*, Montreal, 2013, pp. 131, 132, 419, and Endnote 105 on p. 669) noted that other witnesses at Fort Duquesne failed to mention the "very dubious and unconfirmed story of Indians burning many soldier-captives within sight of Fort Duquesne on the day of Braddock's defeat." Steele suspected Smith "conflated" this tale from other occurrences. Steele concluded: "Smith remembered enough things incorrectly to suggest either a later writing or deliberate errors."
16. August 25, 1755 letter from Virginia Gov. Dinwiddie to Pennsylvania Gov. Morris (*MPCP*, Vol. VI, p. 602).
17. Miller, *Irish Immigrants in the Land of Canaan*, p. 171.
18. Calvin Bricker Jr. and Walter Powell, *Conflict on the Conococheague; 1755-1758*, Mercersburg, Pa., 2009, pp. 24-26.
19. Weslager, *The Delaware Indians*, pp. 246-247.
20. *MPCP*, Vol. VI, p. 641. Weslager, *The Delaware Indians*, p. 227. James H. Merrell, *Into the American Woods, Negotiators on the Pennsylvania Frontier*, New York, 1999, pp. 227-228, 242-243.
21. *MPCP,* Vol. VI, pp. 675-676. Bricker, *Conflict on the Conococheague*, p. 7. Pennsylvania Historic and Museum Commission (PHMC) historical marker for "Big Spring Graveyard" in Fulton County, dedicated 1989.
22. *MPCP,* Vol. VI, pp. 677-680. Isaacson, *Benjamin Franklin* pp. 169-170.
23. Miller, *Irish Immigrants in the Land of Canaan*, p. 172. Bricker, *Conflict on the Conococheague*, pp. 33-36. Franklin's *Pennsylvania Gazette*, Philadelphia, March 18, 1756. Harry E. Foreman, *Fort Loudon Sidelights*, Chambersburg, 1970, pp. 1-5, 41-42.
24. A PHMC historical marker on Pa. Rte. 75, once cited this event, but disappeared. On June 23, 2013, the PHMC erected a new marker at Widow Barr's. However, the latest marker recognizes only another event

at Widow Barr's—the skirmish between British troops and local citizens during the Conococheague uprising of 1765.

25. Bricker, *Conflict on the Conococheague,* pp. 36-39. Indians returned Philip Studebaker at the August 1762 Lancaster Conference. John and Elizabeth Studebaker were among the over 200 captives released as part of the negotiations during Colonel Bouquet's 1764 Ohio expedition. But while John returned home, Elizabeth was one of two girls who escaped back to their Indian families and remained a "white Indian."

26. C. Hale Sipe, *The Indian Wars of Pennsylvania,* Harrisburg, Pa., 1929, p. 273. Bricker, *Conflict on the Conococheague,* pp. 39-42.

27. William H. Egle, *An Illustrated History of the Commonwealth of Pennsylvania,* Philadelphia, 1880, p. 91.

28. *Minutes of the Provincial Council of Pennsylvania (MPCP),* Vol. VII, Harrisburg, 1851, pp. 74-76. Sipe, *The Indian Wars of Pennsylvania,* p. 283.

29. Miller, *Irish Immigrants in the Land of Canaan,* pp. 172-178. The quote is from Jeremiah 12:10.

30. Archibald Loudon, *A Selection of Some of the Most Interesting Narratives of Outrages, Committed by the Indians in their Wars with the White People,* Vol. 1, Carlisle, 1808 (reprinted in Harrisburg, 1888), "A Narrative of the Captivity of John M'cullough, Esq., Written by Himself," pp. 252-301. Sipe, *The Indian Wars of Pennsylvania,* pp. 287-289.

31. Thomas Lynch Montgomery, *Pennsylvania Archives,* Fifth Series, Vol. 1, Harrisburg, 1906, p. 40. Sipe, *The Indian Wars of Pennsylvania,* pp. 304-314. William A. Hunter, *Forts of the Pennsylvania Frontier,* Harrisburg, 1960, pp. 405-410. Ian K. Steele (in *Setting All the Captives Free,* p. 312) wrote that 33 Pennsylvanians and only 14 Delawares were killed during the Kittanning raid. Steele said seven out of 150 white captives were recovered while others say 11 were. Fort Shirley was built on George Croghan's trading post at Aughwick (at present-day Shirleysburg in Huntington County, Pa.). It became a provincial post in December 1755 when Croghan received a captain's commission (Reference: Hunter, *Forts on the Pennsylvania Frontier,* p. 394).

32. Samuel Hazard, *Pennsylvania Archives,* [First Series], Vol. III, Philadelphia, 1853, pp. 40, 51. Sipe, *The Indian Wars of Pennsylvania,* pp. 292-293. Bricker, *Conflict on the Conococheague,* p. 46. In a November 12, 1756, letter to Denny, Armstrong revised the number of casualties near McDowell's to "nineteen people, soldiers, and others kill'd & taken," but in a November 30 letter he noted the loss of soldiers

was due to defections, not murder. (Ref. *Pennsylvania Archives*, [First Series], Vol. III, pp. 51, 78).

33. *Pennsylvania Archives*, [First Series], Vol. III, pp. 58, 83-84. Foreman, *Fort Loudon Sidelights*, pp. 50-59. Hunter, *Forts of the Pennsylvania Frontier*, pp. 435, 463-473, 477. Gary T. Hawbaker, *Fort Loudon on the Frontier*, Hersey, Pa., 1976, p. 40.

34. Bricker, *Conflict on the Conococheague*, pp. 7-8.

35. Hunter, *Forts of the Pennsylvania Frontier*, pp. 133-136.

36. Hunter, *Forts of the Pennsylvania Frontier*, p. 449.

37. Bricker, *Conflict on the Conococheague*, p. 52.

38. Merrell, *Into the American Woods*, pp. 242-247. Nicholas B. Wainwright, *George Croghan, Wilderness Diplomat*, Chapel Hill, N.C., 1959, pp. 150-152. The 1758 Easton Treaty resolved all major Indian grievances with Pennsylvania except those from the infamous Walking Purchase, which were addressed in 1762.

39. "A Narrative of the Captivity of John M'cullough." Steele, *Setting All the Captives Free*, p. 256.

40. Smith, *An Account*, p. 105.

41. Matthew C. Ward, *Breaking the Backcountry, The Seven Years' War in Virginia and Pennsylvania 1754-1765*, Pittsburgh, 2003, pp. 191-193.

42. Ward, *Breaking the Backcountry*, pp. 193-194.

CHAPTER 2   Indians Attack Again: Pontiac's War

43. Francis Jennings, *Empire of Fortune - Crowns, Colonies, and Tribes in the Seven Years War in America*, New York, 1988, pp. 438-441. Ward, *Breaking the Backcountry*, pp. 202-203, 216.

44. Jennings, *Empire of Fortune*, pp. 441-442. Ward, *Breaking the Backcountry*, p. 203. Wainwright, *George Croghan*, 194.

45. Foreman, *Fort Loudon Sidelights*, pp. 2, 61. Wilbur S. Nye, *James Smith, Early Cumberland Valley Patriot*, Carlisle, 1969, p. 9.

46. Ward, *Breaking the Backcountry*, p. 217, *Pennsylvania Gazette*, June 16, 30, July 7, 1763.

47. *Pennsylvania Gazette*, July 21, 1763.

48. *MPCP,* Vol. IX, p. 63.

49. The Royal Proclamation of 1763 also defined new governments for land ceded in the Seven Years War, and gave land grants to officers and soldiers.

50. Smith, *An Account*, p. 108. John Penn was the grandson of William Penn and the son of Richard Penn, who owned a 25% interest in the province, which John eventually inherited.

51. Smith, *An Account*, pp. 106-107.

52. Charles F. Hoban, editor, *Pennsylvania Archives*, Eighth Series, Vol. VI, Harrisburg, 1935, pp. 5437-5438, 5440.

53. *Pennsylvania Archives*, 5th Series, Vol. I, p. 336. Smith, *An Account*, p. 107. Nye, *James Smith*, p. 9.

54. Nye, *James Smith*, pp. 9-10.

55. *Pennsylvania Gazette*, February 9, 1764.

56. Merrell, *Into the American Woods*, pp. 284-287. Kevin Kenny, *Peaceable Kingdom Lost: The Paxton Boys and the Destruction of William Penn's Holy Experiment*, New York, 2009, pp. 1-2, 130-155.

57. Isaacson, *Benjamin Franklin*, p. 213.

58. Kenny, *Peaceable Kingdom Lost*, p. 7.

59. Kenny, *Peaceable Kingdom Lost*, p. 212. While John Armstrong insisted that no one from Cumberland County participated in the Conestoga massacres, Armstrong himself later marched with the Paxton Boys on their way to Philadelphia (Patrick Spero, *Creating Pennsylvania: The Politics of the Frontier and the State, 1682-1800*, University of Pennsylvania Ph.D thesis, 2009, pp. 230, 257 and 268).

60. *Pennsylvania Archives*, Eighth Series, Vol. VI, pp. 5509-5511.

61. *Pennsylvania Archives*, Eighth Series, Vol. VI, pp. 5580-5583. Eleanor M. Webster, "Insurrection at Fort Loudon in 1765—Rebellion or Preservation of Peace?," *Western Pennsylvania Historical Magazine*, April 1964, p. 137.

62. Ward, *Breaking the Backcountry*, pp. 243-244. Louis M. Waddell, *The Papers of Henry Bouquet*, Vol. VI, Harrisburg, 1999, p. 548.

63. Waddell, *The Papers of Henry Bouquet*, Vol. VI, p. 505. In June 1758, Robert Callender was stationed at Fort Loudoun and was in charge of officers and men who repaired Forbes Road from Shippensburg to Fort Littleton (Gary T. Hawbaker, *Fort Loudon on the Frontier*, pp 20-30.) Robert Callender owned a grist mill at the mouth of Letort Spring Run, at Middlesex.

64. *Pennsylvania Gazette,* June 7 and 14, 1764.

65. The June 14, 1764 *Pennsylvania Gazette* contains an extract of a June 5 letter from Fort Loudoun that said the initial attack killing 13 was "four miles down the creek" from the fort, whereas a June 6, 1765 letter from John Armstrong in Carlisle (*Pennsylvania Archives*, First Series,

Vol. 4, pp. 175-176) said the attack was "four miles South of Fort Loudoun." The latter places the attack about a mile northeast of present-day Mercersburg and the former places it about one and a third miles west of present-day Lemasters if we interpret mileage "down the creek" to be downstream and along the winding West Branch of Conococheague Creek. The June 14, 1764 *Pennsylvania Gazette* also contains an extract of a June 6, 1764 letter from Carlisle that discusses the sad fate of the captives.

66. *MPCP,* Vol. IX, pp. 190-192. *Pennsylvania Gazette*, July 12, 1764. Isaacson, *Benjamin Franklin*, p. 213.

67. *MPCP,* Vol. IX, pp. 190-192. *Pennsylvania Gazette*, July 12, 1764.

68. *Pennsylvania Gazette*, August 9, 1764.

69. "John McCullough Narrative," p. 471.

70. *Pennsylvania Gazette*, August 9, 1764.

71. *Pennsylvania Gazette*, August 9 and 30, 1764.

72. "John McCullough Narrative," p. 471. The Indians scalped Archie McCullough, but he became the sole survivor of the Enoch Brown School massacre. He was the cousin of the Indian captive, John McCullough. (Reference: Bricker, *Conflict on the Conococheague*, pp. 56-58).

73. Waddell, *The Papers of Henry Bouquet*, Vol. VI, pp. 548, 574.

74. Waddell, *The Papers of Henry Bouquet* Vol. VI, pp. 576-577, 602-603.

75. Waddell, *The Papers of Henry Bouquet*, Vol. VI, p. 608.

76. *Pennsylvania Archives*, First Series, Vol. 4, pp. 199-200, 206. Waddell, *The Papers of Henry Bouquet*, Vol. VI, pp. 602, 631. Cyrus Cort, *Col. Henry Bouquet and his Campaigns of 1763 and 1764*, Lancaster, Pa., 1883, p. 62.

77. *Pennsylvania Gazette*, September 13, 27, 1764.

78. Gregory Evans Dowd, *War Under Heaven: Pontiac, the Indian Nations & the British Empire*, Baltimore, 2002, pp. 162-163. Nye, *James Smith*, p. 12. Smith, *An Account*, p. 107. James Smith, *A Treatise on the Mode and Manner of Indian War*, reprinted Chicago, 1948 (originally published in Paris, Kentucky, 1812), pp. 50, 53.

79. Dowd, *War Under Heaven*, pp. 162-166. Steele, *Setting All the Captives Free*, p. 337. *MPCP*, Vol. IX, p. 238.

80. Smith, *A Treatise*, pp. 49-50.

81. Smith, *An Account*, p. 108. Ian K. Steele (in *Setting All the Captives Free*, pp. 179 and 180) wrote that the Fort Pitt hostages consisted of six Delawares, six Shawnees, and two Mingos. All except three of the

Delawares escaped. It is noteworthy that James Smith and later Governor Penn's council cited concern only about the escape of the Shawnee hostages. Perhaps that was because the Shawnees still held white captives. However, it is also noteworthy that all except one of 42 captives the Shawnees delivered to Fort Pitt in May 1765 were taken from Virginia (Steele, *Setting All the Captives Free*, p. 337).

82. Waddell, *The Papers of Henry Bouquet*, Vol. VI, p. 737. Patrick Griffin, *American Leviathan: Empire, Nation, and Revolutionary Frontier*, New York, 2007, pp. 70-71.

83. *Pennsylvania Gazette*, November 15, 1764.

84. Waddell, *The Papers of Henry Bouquet*, Vol. VI, pp. 736, 738.

85. Webster, "Insurrection at Fort Loudoun in 1765," p. 128. Robert G. Crist, "Cumberland County," in John B. Frantz and William Pencak, editors, *Beyond Philadelphia: The American Revolution in the Pennsylvania Hinterland*, University Park, Pa., 1998, p. 112.

86. Dowd, *War Under Heaven*, p. 165.

87. *MPCP*, Vol. IX, pp. 238-239.

88. Wainwright, *George Croghan*, pp. 4, 112-113, 190.

89. Wainwright, *George Croghan*, pp. 200-207.

90. Wainwright, George Croghan, pp. 212-213.

91. Wainwright, George Croghan, pp. 9, 48.

92. Wainwright, *George Croghan*, pp. 213-215.

93. Waddell, *The Papers of Henry Bouquet*, Vol. VI, p. 748.

94. Wainwright, *George Croghan*, pp. 213-215.

95. *Thomas Gage Papers*, microfiche copies at the Pennsylvania Archives in Harrisburg, Pa., from original documents in University of Michigan's Clements Library, Deposition of James Maxwell, April 3, 1765; Deposition of Robert Callender, March 28, 1765; Deposition of Robert Allison, April 1, 1765.

96. *Thomas Gage Papers*, Deposition of James Maxwell, April 3, 1765.

97. *Pennsylvania Archives*, First Series, Vol. 4, p. 237.

CHAPTER 3   Ambush at Sideling Hill: March & April 1765

98. Bradford's *Pennsylvania Journal*, Philadelphia, March 21, 1765. The March 14 letter was also published in the *Maryland Gazette*, April 4, 1765. The description of the recruitment advertisements' content is different from the one Thomas Romberg claimed to have found on May 29, 1765.

99. *Thomas Gage Papers*, Deposition of Elias Davison, March 8, 1765; Depositions of Robert Allison, March 10 and April 1, 1765.

100. *Pennsylvania Journal*, March 28, 1765.

101. Fulton County Historical Society, McConnellsburg, *200 Years of Quiet Progression*, McConnellsburg, Pa., 1986, p. 9. According to *Old Mercersburg* (p. 51): "in 1761, the people of Peters township petitioned for a road, saying that they have no prospect of a standing market for the produce of the country except at Baltimore, and flour being the principal commodity, this 'township produceth and having two mills in said township, viz: John McDowell's and William Smith's,' they pray the Court to 'appoint men to view and lay out a road from each of said mills to meet at or near the house of William Maxwell and from thence to run by the nearest and best way towards the said town of Baltimore.' The viewers reported in favor of granting this petition but the branch roads to the mills were restricted to bridle paths which were to unite near James Irwin's mill in Peters township, and thence through Antrim township to Nicholson's Gap in the South Mountain, and from there to Baltimore."

102. *Thomas Gage Papers*, Deposition of Elias Davison, March 8, 1765; Deposition of Robert Allison, March 10, 1765.

103. *Thomas Gage Papers*, Deposition of Elias Davison, March 8, 1765; Depositions of Robert Allison, April 1, 1765.

104. *Thomas Gage Papers*, Deposition of William Smith, April 3, 1765.

105. Waddell, *The Papers of Henry Bouquet*, Vol. VI, pp. 711, 764. (Note 4). One indication of the number of men garrisoned at Fort Loudoun under Lieutenant Eddingstone is that he received 30 new blankets for his men stationed there (Hawbaker, *Fort Loudon on the Frontier*, p. 52).

106. *Thomas Gage Papers*, Deposition of William Smith, April 3, 1765.

107. Smith, *An Account,* p. 108.

108. Presumably Cunningham's tavern was "the old rough tavern on the Run" mentioned in *Old Mercersburg*, p. 37. The site was also the birthplace of Governor (and U.S. Senator) William Findlay, as noted by a historical marker at the Liberty gas station. The authenticity of William Smith's house was largely based on "W. S." carved into its cornerstone (*Old Mercersburg*, p. 35). Additional evidence dating the house to the mid-eighteenth century came from architectural reviews and archeological evidence. A more precise way of dating the house would be a tree-ring analysis of its floor beams, which currently are

stored along with stones and other items, waiting for the house's reconstruction.

109. *Thomas Gage Papers*, Deposition of Robert Allison, March 10, 1765. The McConnell House is on the National Register of Historic Places. Its nomination form dates it to "circa 1760."

110. Smith, *An Account*, p. 110.

111. *Thomas Gage Papers*, Deposition of Robert Allison, March 10, 1765; Deposition of Elias Davison, March 8, 1765.

112. *Pennsylvania Journal*, March 28, 1765. *Thomas Gage Papers*, Deposition of Robert Allison, March 10, 1765.

113. A map in Nye, *James Smith* (pp. 18-19) shows the packhorse trail roughly following US Route 522 north from McConnellsburg.

114. *Thomas Gage Papers*, Deposition of Robert Allison, March 10, 1765. Waddell, *The Papers of Henry Bouquet*, Vol. VI, pp. 764-765.

115. Smith, *An Account*, pp. 110-111.

116. Griffin, *American Leviathan*, p. 76. *Thomas Gage Papers*, Deposition of Robert Allison, April 1, 1765.

117. *Pennsylvania Archives*, First Series, Vol. 4, pp. 231, 240.

118. *Pennsylvania Archives*, First Series, Vol. 4, pp. 234-235.

119. *Pennsylvania Archives*, First Series, Vol. 4, p. 235. Although McGlashan never named the mountain gap, it is reasonable to assume it was the same one the packhorse trains and the locals passed through on their way to Great Cove. Those who participated in the Sideling Hill attack obviously were not in a hurry to get home, being still on the packhorse trail at midnight.

120. *Thomas Gage Papers*, Deposition of Robert Allison, March 10, 1765. Waddell, *The Papers of Henry Bouquet*, Vol. VI, p. 763. *Pennsylvania Journal*, Philadelphia, March 21, 1765.

121. Waddell, *The Papers of Henry Bouquet*, Vol. VI, pp. 767-768.

122. *Thomas Gage Papers*, Deposition of Robert Allison, March 10, 1765.

123. *Pennsylvania Archives*, First Series, Vol. 4, pp. 235-236. *Thomas Gage Papers*, March 9, 1765 letter from Grant to Bouquet. McGlashan's deposition is unclear whether four or five prisoners were taken on his return trip from Sideling Hill, but Grant's letter specifically says one was taken and then three more, for a total of four. (Note that the transcription of Grant's letter on page 763 of Waddell, *The Papers of Henry Bouquet*, Vol. VI is slightly different. The latter incorrectly and confusingly says "fellow prisoner <u>Will</u> three More of the Said party" rather than "fellow prisoner <u>with</u> three More of the Said party.").

124. Waddell, *The Papers of Henry Bouquet*, Vol. VI, p. 763.
125. *Thomas Gage Papers*, Deposition of James Maxwell, April 3, 1765.
126. Waddell, *The Papers of Henry Bouquet*, Vol. VI, p. 763.
127. *Pennsylvania Archives*, First Series, Vol. 4, p. 220.
128. *Thomas Gage Papers*, March 11, 1765, letter from Capt. Thomas Barnsley in Carlisle to Thomas Gage. Waddell, *The Papers of Henry Bouquet*, Vol. VI, pp. 765, 777. *Pennsylvania Archives*, First Series, Vol. 4, pp. 245.
129. *Thomas Gage Papers*, Deposition of James Maxwell, Apr. 3, 1765.
130. Smith, *An Account*, p. 110.
131. March 14, 1765 *Bradford Journal*. *Thomas Gage Papers*, Deposition of James Maxwell, April 3, 1765.
132. *Thomas Gage Papers*, Deposition of Richard Brownson, April 3, 1765; Deposition of James Maxwell, April 3, 1765. The border between Pennsylvania and Maryland was still unsettled in 1765, the year Mason and Dixon began their survey of that line.
133. *Pennsylvania Journal*, March 28, 1765.
134. *Thomas Gage Papers*, Deposition of James Maxwell, April 3, 1765. The fact that Callender had 19 or 20 wagon loads at Howe's after delivering only 16 or 17 in his first shipment the previous winter, and having since shipped out over 117 packhorse loads from there, shows that he shipped and stored other goods from Philadelphia at Howe's.
135. *Thomas Gage Papers*, Croghan at Fort Pitt to Gage, March 12, 1765. Waddell, *The Papers of Henry Bouquet*, Vol. VI, pp. 766-777. Many of Croghan's letters, like this one to Bouquet, contain horrible spelling. But the one written to Gage that same day does not. Perhaps Croghan had others write some of his letters.
136. *Thomas Gage Papers*, March 16, 1765 letter from Gage to Capt. Thomas Barnsley.
137. *Pennsylvania Archives*, First Series, Vol. 4, pp. 214-216, Waddell, *The Papers of Henry Bouquet*, Vol. VI, p. 779, Wainwright, *George Croghan*, pp. 216-217.
138. Wainwright, *George Croghan*, pp. 216-217. *Thomas Gage Papers*, June 9, 1765 letter from Thomas Gage to John Reid.
139. Waddell, *The Papers of Henry Bouquet* Vol. VI, p. 765.
140. Smith, *An Account*, p. 113. *Pennsylvania Archives*, First Series, Vol. 4, pp. 219-220, 224-225, 228.
141. *Pennsylvania Archives*, First Series, Vol. 4, pp. 224-225.
142. *Pennsylvania Archives*, First Series, Vol. 4, p. 220.
143. *Pennsylvania Archives*, First Series, Vol. 4, p. 220.

144. Waddell, *The Papers of Henry Bouquet*, Volume VI, pp. 777-779.
145. *MPCP*, Vol. IX, p. 275.
146. This author could not find exact dates for Penn's visit to Carlisle. In an April 10, 1765 letter from Bouquet to Penn (Waddell, *The Papers of Henry Bouquet*, Volume VI, p. 780), Bouquet noted that Penn had returned to Philadelphia, so he probably left Carlisle in early April. In Carlisle, depositions of witnesses were taken on March 28 and April 1 and 3. The grand jury was held on April 16, 1765, based on a May 20, 1765 letter from John Ross to Benjamin Franklin in which Ross said it was held on "the third Tuesday in last month" (*The Papers of Benjamin Franklin*, Sponsored by The American Philosophical Society and Yale University, http://franklinpapers.org/franklin//). The quote is from Theodore Thayer, *Pennsylvania Politics and the Growth of Democracy, 1740-1776*, Harrisburg, Pa., 1953, p. 88.
147. May 20, 1765 letter from John Ross to Benjamin Franklin (*The Papers of Benjamin Franklin*).
148. *The Papers of Benjamin Franklin*, May 27 1765, letter from Samuel Wharton to Franklin. Eleanor M. Webster wrote (in "Insurrection at Fort Loudon in 1765," pp. 131, 138) that the goods of Baynton, Wharton and Morgan were illegal because the firm was not licensed for trade. If that was true, then their license must have been only temporarily revoked because it seems unlikely that an established mercantile firm could operate illegally for long.

CHAPTER 4   Gunfight at Widow Barr's: May, June & July 1765

149. *The Papers of Benjamin Franklin*, May 27 1765 letter from Samuel Wharton to Franklin. *Pennsylvania Archives*, First Series, Vol. 4, p. 225. In regards to whether Spear's convoy had a an escort, one merchant wrote: "one Speer, a sutler, having provided sundry necessaries for the officers at Pittsburg and the intermediate posts, wrote to the Commanding officer, who sent him a serjeant and 12 men as an escort. In confidence of this guard, he takes sundry goods to trade with the Indians, and arrives safe at fort Loudon" (*The Papers of Benjamin Franklin*, A Letter from a Merchant in Philadelphia, to his Correspondent in London, dated June 19, 1765). However, this author suspects the letter writer might have confused the mission of the 13-man squad of Fort Loudoun troops after the goods arrived as being an escort before it arrived.
150. *The Papers of Benjamin Franklin*, May 27 1765 letter from Samuel

Wharton to Franklin. *MPCP,* Vol. IX, p. 269. Foreman, *Fort Loudoun Sidelights,* pp. 13-14, 62, 69.

151. *Pennsylvania Archives,* First Series, Vol. 4, p. 233.

152. *Pennsylvania Archives,* First Series, Vol. 4, p. 222. John Shelby was the brother of the famous frontiersman, Evan Shelby, Jr.

153. *Pennsylvania Archives,* First Series, Vol. 4, pp. 233-234.

154. McGlashan failed to identify his prisoner. Wilbur Nye said that man was James Brown, who McGlashan shot in the thigh, and who lived at the entrance to Cowan's Gap. (Nye, *James Smith,* p. 17, Endnote 67 on p. 32. Also Foreman, *Fort Loudoun Highlights,* pp. 69, 71).

155. *Pennsylvania Archives,* First Series, Vol. 4, pp. 222-223.

156. *Pennsylvania Archives,* First Series, Vol. 4, p. 224.

157. *Pennsylvania Archives,* First Series, Vol. 4, p. 229.

158. *Pennsylvania Archives,* First Series, Vol. 4, p. 232. A gunshot wound to the thigh could be fatal if the femoral artery was severed.

159. *Pennsylvania Archives,* First Series, Vol. 4, pp. 220-221. It is interesting that Grant said he had showed orders "from Brigadier General Bouquet for permitting Goods to pass" on May 10, 1765. General Gage wrote to Colonel Bouquet on May 15, 1765, five days later, telling him of his promotion to brigadier general (Waddell, *The Papers of Henry Bouquet,* Vol. VI, p. 789).

160. *Pennsylvania Archives,* First Series, Vol. 4, p. 270.

161. *Pennsylvania Archives,* First Series, Vol. 4, p. 225. Eleanor M. Webster (in "Insurrection at Fort Loudon in 1765," p. 134) said that this Justice William Allen was the "Chief Justice of the province." This author, however, wonders if the chief justice in Philadelphia would have handled such a case, and whether there might have been a magistrate in Cumberland County with the same name.

162. Wainwright, *George Croghan,* p. 219.

163. *MPCP,* Vol. IX, pp. 249-264.

164. *The Papers of Benjamin Franklin,* A Letter from a Merchant in Philadelphia, to his Correspondent in London, dated June 19, 1765.

165. *Pennsylvania Archives,* First Series, Vol. 4, pp. 220-222.

166. *Thomas Gage Papers,* June 7, 1765 letter from John Reid to Gage.

167. *Pennsylvania Archives,* First Series, Vol. 4, pp. 229-230.

168. *Pennsylvania Archives,* First Series, Vol. 4, p. 232.

169. *Pennsylvania Archives,* First Series, Vol. 4, p. 232.

170. *MPCP,* Vol. IX, p. 270.

171. *MPCP,* Vol. IX, pp. 249-264.

172. *MPCP,* Vol. IX, pp. 264-266.
173. *MPCP,* Vol. IX, pp. 277-280.
174. *The Benjamin Franklin Papers,* July 16, 1765 letter from Thomas Wharton to Franklin.
175. *Pennsylvania Archives,* First Series, Vol. 4, p. 237.
176. Isaacson, *Benjamin Franklin,* pp. 217-220. *The Benjamin Franklin Papers,* June 8, 1765 letter from Franklin to John Ross.
177. *Pennsylvania Archives,* First Series, Vol. 4, pp. 238-239.
178. *MPCP,* Vol. IX, p. 271.
179. *Pennsylvania Archives,* First Series, Vol. 4, pp. 237-239.
180. *Thomas Gage Papers,* June 9, 1765 letter from Gage to Reid.
181. *MPCP,* Vol. IX, pp. 267-271.
182. *MPCP,* Vol. IX, pp. 273-274.
183. *MPCP,* Vol. IX pp. 272-277, 281.
184. *Pennsylvania Archives,* First Series, Vol. 4, pp. 237, 244.
185. *Pennsylvania Archives,* First Series, Vol. 4, p. 241.
186. *Pennsylvania Archives,* First Series, Vol. 4, p. 231.
187. *Pennsylvania Archives,* First Series, Vol. 4, pp. 231, 232.
188. Wainwright, *George Croghan,* pp. 219-221.
189. Wainwright, *George Croghan,* pp. 221-223.
190. Wainwright, *George Croghan,* pp. 223-225.

CHAPTER 5   Siege at Fort Loudoun: November 1765 & Beyond

191. *Pennsylvania Archives,* First Series, Vol. 4, pp. 246-247.
192. *Pennsylvania Archives,* First Series, Vol. 4, pp. 247-248. Archeological excavations made at the Fort Loudoun site in the late 1970s and early 1980s found the foundation for Mathew Patton's second house (the first was burned by Indians) within the lines of post molds marking where the stockade of the fort had been.
193. *Pennsylvania Archives,* First Series, Vol. 4, pp. 245-246.
194. *Pennsylvania Archives,* First Series, Vol. 4, pp. 245-246. Patrick Spero (in *Creating Pennsylvania,* p. 269) cited a December 18, 1765, letter from Penn to William Smith and John Reynolds in which Penn said it was his "pleasure" to allow the guns be returned "forthwith . . . to their respective owners."
195. *MPCP,* Vol. IX, p. 292.
196. *MPCP,* Vol. IX, pp. 292-293.
197. *MPCP,* Vol. IX, pp. 293, 297.

198. *MPCP,* Vol. IX, pp. 300, 301.
199. *MPCP,* Vol. IX, p. 302.
200. *MPCP,* Vol. IX, p. 304.
201. *MPCP,* Vol. IX, p. 303.
202. Kenny, *Peaceable Kingdom Lost,* pp. 211-214.
203. Crist, "Cumberland County," pp. 123, 177.
204. *Old Mercersburg,* pp. 26, 29.

CHAPTER 6   Not a Rebellion: Summary and Conclusions

205. *Pennsylvania Archives,* First Series, Vol. 4, pp. 220-222. *MPCP,* Vol. IX, pp. 273-274.
206. Webster, "Insurrection at Fort Loudoun in 1765," pp. 137-138. The definition of rebellion was from *Webster's II New College Dictionary,* Boston, 1999.
207. Greg Dowd (in *War Under Heaven,* p. 204) made the case for James Smith's compassion towards neutral Indians. However, Patrick Griffin (in *American Leviathan,* p. 295 Endnote 26) refuted Dowd's conclusion, implying that the Black Boys were among those Sir William Johnson called "parties, threatening to destroy all the Indians they met, or all white people who dealt with them."

References

The American Philosophical Society and Yale University, *The Papers of Benjamin Franklin*, http://franklinpapers.org/franklin//

Bradford's *Pennsylvania Journal*, Philadelphia

Cyrus Cort, *Col. Henry Bouquet and his Campaigns of 1763 and 1764*, Lancaster, Pa., 1883

Robert G. Crist, "Cumberland County," in John B. Frantz and William Pencak, editors, *Beyond Philadelphia: The American Revolution in the Pennsylvania Hinterland*, University Park, Pa., 1998, pp. 107-132

Gregory Evans Dowd, *War Under Heaven—Pontiac, the Indian Nations & the British Empire,* Baltimore, 2002

William H. Egle, *An Illustrated History of the Commonwealth of Pennsylvania*, Philadelphia, 1880

Harry E. Foreman, *Fort Loudon Sidelights*, Chambersburg, Pa., 1970

Franklin's *Pennsylvania Gazette*, Philadelphia

Gary T. Hawbaker, *Fort Loudon on the Frontier,* Hershey, Pa., 1976

Samuel Hazard, editor, *Pennsylvania Archives*, [First Series], Vol. III, Philadelphia, 1853

Charles F. Hoban, editor, *Pennsylvania Archives*, Eighth Series, Vol. VI, Harrisburg, 1935

William A. Hunter, *Forts of the Pennsylvania Frontier*, Harrisburg, 1960

Walter Isaacson, *Benjamin Franklin, An American Life*, New York, 2003

Kevin Kenny, *Peaceable Kingdom Lost: The Paxton Boys and the Destruction of William Penn's Holy Experiment*, New York, 2009

Archibald Loudon, *A Selection of Some of the Most Interesting Narratives of Outrages, Committed by the Indians in their Wars with the White People*, Vol. 1, Carlisle, 1808 (reprinted in Harrisburg, 1888)

I. H. McCauley, *Historical Sketch of Franklin County, Pennsylvania*, Chambersburg, Pa., 1878

James H. Merrell, *Into the American Woods, Negotiators on the Pennsylvania Frontier*, New York, 1999

Kerby A. Miller, Arnold Schrier, Bruce D. Doling, David N. Doyle, editors, *Irish Immigrants in the Land of Canaan*, New York, 2003, Chapter 21, "James McCullough 1748-1758"

Minutes of the Provincial Council of Pennsylvania, Vol. VI, Harrisburg, 1851

Minutes of the Provincial Council of Pennsylvania, Vol. VII, Harrisburg, 1851

Minutes of the Provincial Council of Pennsylvania, Vol. IX, Harrisburg, 1852

Thomas Lynch Montgomery, *Pennsylvania Archives*, Fifth Series, Vol. I, Harrisburg, 1906

Wilbur S. Nye, *James Smith, Early Cumberland Valley Patriot*, Carlisle, Pa., 1969
John Graham Palmer, *The Palmer Papers*, unpublished with copies at the Conococheague Institute library

James D. Rice, *Nature & History in the Potomac Country*, Baltimore, 2009

G. O. Seilhamer, *The Bard Family*, Chambersburg, Pa., 1908

C. Hale Sipe, *The Indian Wars of Pennsylvania*, Harrisburg, Pa., 1929

James Smith, *An Account of the Remarkable Occurrences in the Life and Travels of Col. James Smith*, reprinted Cincinnati, 1870 (originally published in Lexington, Kentucky, 1799)

James Smith, *A Treatise on the Mode and Manner of Indian War*, reprinted Chicago, 1948 (originally published in Paris, Kentucky, 1812)

Patrick Spero, *Creating Pennsylvania: The Politics of the Frontier and the State, 1682-1800*, University of Pennsylvania PhD Thesis, 2009

Ian K. Steele, *Setting All the Captives Free: Capture, Adjustment, and Recollection in Allegheny Country*, Montreal, 2013

Theodore Thayer, *Pennsylvania Politics and the Growth of Democracy, 1740-1776*, Harrisburg, Pa., 1953

Louis M. Waddell, *The Papers of Henry Bouquet*, Vol. VI, Harrisburg, 1999

Nicholas B. Wainwright, *George Croghan, Wilderness Diplomat*, Chapel Hill, N.C., 1959

Matthew C. Ward, *Breaking the Backcountry, The Seven Years' War in Virginia and Pennsylvania 1754-1765*, Pittsburgh, 2003

Warner, Beers & Company, *History of Franklin County, Pennsylvania*, Chicago, 1887

Eleanor M. Webster, "Insurrection at Fort Loudon in 1765—Rebellion or Preservation of Peace?" *Western Pennsylvania Historical Magazine*, April 1964, pp. 125-139

Woman's Club of Mercersburg, *Old Mercersburg*, New York, 1912

Index

45010716R00096

Made in the USA
San Bernardino, CA
29 January 2017